DEC 0 9 2011

Protecting
Earth's
Food Supply

Radicchio 4.99 lb.

Baby Bok Choy 1.99 lb.

ENVIRONMENT AT RISK

Protecting Earth's Food Supply

CHRISTINE PETERSEN

mc Marshall Cavendish
Benchmark
New York

Published by Marshall Cavendish Benchmark
An imprint of Marshall Cavendish Corporation

This publication represents the opinions and views of the author based on Christine Petersen's personal experience, knowledge, and research. The information in this book serves as a general guide only. The author and publisher have used their best efforts in preparing this book and disclaim liability rising directly and indirectly from the use and application of this book.

Other Marshall Cavendish Offices:
Marshall Cavendish International (Asia) Private Limited, 1 New Industrial Road, Singapore 536196 • Marshall Cavendish International (Thailand) Co Ltd. 253 Asoke, 12th Flr, Sukhumvit 21 Road, Klongtoey Nua, Wattana, Bangkok 10110, Thailand • Marshall Cavendish (Malaysia) Sdn Bhd, Times Subang, Lot 46, Subang Hi-Tech Industrial Park, Batu Tiga, 40000 Shah Alam, Selangor Darul Ehsan, Malaysia

Marshall Cavendish is a trademark of Times Publishing Limited

All websites were available and accurate when this book was sent to press.

Library of Congress Cataloging-in-Publication Data
Petersen, Christine.
Protecting earth's food supply / by Christine Petersen.
p. cm. — (Environment at risk)
Includes bibliographical references and index.
Summary: "Provides comprehensive information on Earth's food supply and its protection, the interrelationships of the natural world, environmental problems both natural and man-made, the relative risks associated with these problems, and solutions for resolving and/or preventing them"—Provided by publisher.
ISBN 978-0-7614-4008-6
1. Food. 2. Foodborne diseases. 3. Food contamination. 4. Food—Safety measures. I. Title.
RA601.P48 2010
363.19'26—dc22
2008035949

Editor: Christine Florie
Publisher: Michelle Bisson
Art Director: Anahid Hamparian
Series Designer: Sonia Chaghatzbanian

Expert Reader: Dr. Dean O. Cliver, Professor Emeritus of Food Safety, University of California, Davis

Photo research by Marybeth Kavanagh

Cover photo by Andy Sacks/Stone/Getty Images

The photographs in this book are used by permission and through the courtesy of:
Getty Images: Tom Hopkins/Aurora, 2–3 (top); Peter Essick/Aurora, 23; Akira Kaede/Photodisc, 2 (bottom); Jodi Cobb/National Geographic, 13; Joseph J. Scherschel/National Geographic, 29; Teubner/Stockfood Creative, 30; Nigel Cattlin/Visuals Unlimited, 33; Rischgitz, 37; Kevin Summers/Photographer's Choice, 42; Graeme Norways/Stone, 70; AP Photo: 61, 63; Toby Talbot, 6; Kevork Djansezian, 11; Tampa Tribune-News Channel 8, Paul Lamison, 19; The News & Advance, R. David Duncan III, 48; Photoedit, Inc.: David Young Wolff, 9; Jeff Greenberg, 26; David Snyder, 46; Alamy: Phil Degginger, 18; Bon Appetit, 20; PHOTOTAKE Inc., 25; Art Resource: HIP, 34, 56; Minden Pictures: Tim Fitzharris, 39; The Bridgeman Art Library: British Museum, London, UK, 44; akg-images: 54; The Granger Collection: 68; The Image Works: Janet Wishnetsky/Impact/HIP, 72; Superstock: J.Silver, 74; Uppercut Images, 76; Alamy: Jeff Morgan food and drink, 80; Steve Skjold, 82

Printed in Malaysia (T)
1 3 5 6 4 2

Contents

One
Outbreak

It's always exciting to drag the grill out of the garage for that first spring barbeque. Once a few burgers are cooking, memories of dark winter days seem to quickly fade away. In the spring of 2008 many backyard grills were fired up as usual. As Americans prepared their garnishes, salads, and side dishes, however, those who paid attention to the news began to leave one item off the menu: tomatoes.

In April 2008 the Centers for Disease Control and Prevention (CDC) received multiple reports of *Salmonella* infections. These bacteria live in the intestines of humans and a wide variety of animals, including cows, pigs, chickens, and domestic animals. Like many pathogens (bacteria, viruses, fungi, and parasites), *Salmonella* is transmitted by feces. Once food items are contaminated, several mistakes in the kitchen can lead to infection:

- undercooking meats and eggs

- leaving foods out of the refrigerator for too long

In April 2008 a salmonellosis outbreak in the United States was initially linked to tomatoes.

A Good Defense

It can be difficult to prevent food-borne illnesses, even when strong government regulations are in place. A good starting point is for every person to understand how pathogens are transmitted. There are four common routes.

1. Direct contact: pathogens move from person to person or between animals and people. This often happens when people don't wash their hands after using the bathroom.

2. Vehicles: food or water may carry pathogens. People become ill after consuming the vehicle.

3. Vectors: animals can act as vectors. In a nonfood example, many ticks carry *Borrelia burgdorferi* bacteria. Their bite transmits the bacteria, which causes Lyme disease in humans.

4. Aerosols: airborne particles can contain pathogens. They may be produced when an infected person coughs, sneezes, or vomits, or from the dust of dried feces. They may be breathed in; aerosols also land on surfaces and then are transferred by direct contact.

In sports it is said that the best defense is a strong offense. Hand washing is the number-one best personal strategy for the prevention of food-borne illnesses.

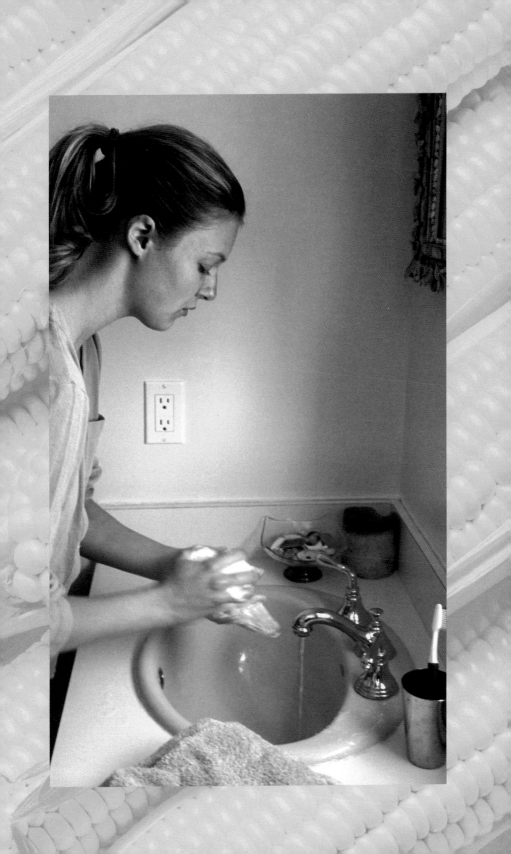

- failing to wash fruits and vegetables before cooking or eating

- poor hand washing before cooking or eating

There may be no sign of infection for three to five days. Then it hits: fever, nausea, stomach pain, and diarrhea (with or without blood). Aside from providing fluids and getting rest, there is no treatment for salmonellosis (illness or infection caused by *Salmonella*). Healthy adults usually recover in less than a week—though it won't be a week they'll soon forget. Infections are much more serious for children, the elderly, and people whose immune systems are already weakened. Severe *Salmonella* infections in these people can result in kidney failure or even death.

The earliest cases of salmonellosis were scattered across several states that are geographically widespread: Arizona, Colorado, Idaho, Illinois, Indiana, Kansas, and Utah. At first there was no obvious connection between them. Then a clue came in mid–May, when a cluster of infections popped up simultaneously at the Northern Navajo Medical Center in New Mexico. Approximately 2,300 strains (different genetic types) of *Salmonella* are known, and two of these are responsible for about half of all cases of salmonellosis. The sick people lived on different parts of the large Navajo reservation, but lab analysis revealed that they all had an uncommon strain called *Salmonella* Saintpaul. The April infections in other states were analyzed and found to be from the Saintpaul strain as well. Although the victims were not related to one another, health officials now knew that the source of their illnesses was—somehow.

Outbreak

Food-borne infections often occur independently or in small clusters; for example when a family eats food that has sat out of the refrigerator for too long. But once in a while a major contamination takes place that affects many people. This is called an outbreak. In 2008 all the signs pointed to an outbreak of salmonellosis. In order to reduce the impact, experts had to take two steps: conduct a traceback investigation to identify the source and inform the public about risks and prevention methods. Experts from the Indian Health Service and CDC started the traceback investigation on the Navajo reservation. A lengthy series of interviews was conducted to figure out what foods the victims had eaten before getting sick. Tomatoes were the one item that came up in all these interviews.

In the decade prior to 2008 tomatoes had been linked to twelve outbreaks of food-borne illnesses. It looked like they were once again involved, so in early June the U.S. Food and Drug Administration (FDA) sent out a nationwide notice. The public was warned about the possibility of *Salmonella*

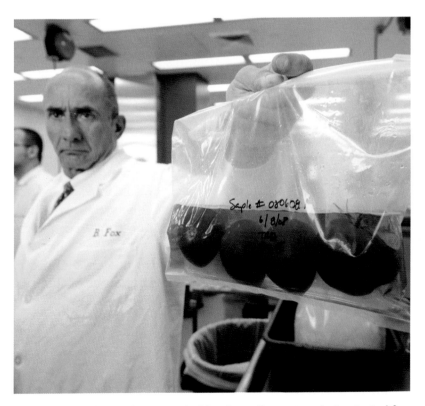

A U.S. Food and Drug inspector holds a bag of tomatoes being tested for *Salmonella* in June 2008.

infection and advised to avoid three types of large tomatoes. For weeks Americans avoided this staple food. Retailers pulled many tomatoes from their shelves, restaurants left them off their menus, and boxes of tomatoes sat unsold in warehouses. Meanwhile, investigators worked at breakneck speed to locate the source of the infected produce. This stage of the traceback is important because contamination can take place anywhere on the food supply chain: in the fields from manure, from water that is used to irrigate or wash the produce, and from infected workers in fields, warehouses, stores, or restaurants.

Investigators began by visiting the same stores and restaurants used by people who had gotten sick. This led to tomato suppliers. Suppliers provided information about their tomato distributors. Then distributors listed the farms where they obtained tomatoes. Investigators were surprised and frustrated to learn that up to 90 percent of tomatoes are routinely moved into different crates at distribution centers. This process, called repacking, means that tomatoes from different farms are mixed up once they reach a store or restaurant. As a result, it's virtually impossible to track tomatoes back to the farms where they were grown. Investigators did learn that the suspect types of tomatoes were all distributed during the same time period from two major locations: Florida and Mexico. Tomatoes, soil, and water were sampled from farms in both locations. No infectious source could be found, and the number of illnesses continued to increase nationwide.

Then an unexpected pattern began to emerge. Clusters of salmonellosis were identified among people who ate at Mexican restaurants, first in Texas and then in several other states. Patrons of a natural foods restaurant in Minnesota became ill as well. The investigation showed no consistent link to tomatoes—but the sick people had all eaten salsa containing raw jalapeño or serrano chili peppers. These were traced to two farms in Mexico, both of which exported their produce to the United States

By late summer 2008 it was determined that chili peppers from Mexico were the cause of the *Salmonella* outbreak in the United States.

through the same packing plant. The CDC was finally able to say with confidence that raw chili peppers were the vehicle for transmission of the *Salmonella* bacteria. The supply chain that brought these peppers into the United States was stopped, and in late August the outbreak gradually ended. Although the cluster of illnesses on the Navajo reservation was never fully connected to these peppers, it is possible that the victims ate tomatoes that also were processed through this plant.

During the 2008 outbreak more than 1,440 cases of *Salmonella* Saintpaul infection were reported in forty-three states and Washington, D.C. Before its conclusion almost three hundred people had been hospitalized, and two deaths were linked to the bacteria. Yet this number is probably only

a fraction of those who were actually impacted. According to the CDC:

> Because many ill persons do not seek attention, and of those that do, many are not tested, many cases of foodborne illness go undiagnosed. For example, CDC estimates that 38 cases of salmonellosis actually occur for every case that is actually diagnosed and reported to public health authorities.

Based on this formula the number of cases may have been closer to 55,000, making this one of the largest *Salmonella* outbreaks ever transmitted by produce.

Two
Food Hazards

The United Nations' World Health Organization (WHO) defines food-borne illnesses as "diseases, either infectious or toxic in nature, caused by agents that enter the body through the ingestion of food." The organization adds a stern warning: "Every person is at risk of food-borne illness." WHO has statistics to back up this claim; they report that 1.8 million people die each year from illnesses caused by consuming contaminated food or water. People may be most vulnerable to food-borne illnesses if they live in regions that can't afford water or sewage treatment systems—but citizens of wealthier nations aren't immune. According to the FDA, 76 million Americans contract food-borne illnesses each year, and five thousand deaths result.

Food scientists describe three broad categories of food safety hazards: microbiological, chemical, and physical. Microbiological hazards are pathogens: bacteria, viruses, fungi, and parasites (usually either microscopic protozoa or worms). Chemical hazards include a wide variety of natural toxins and man-made chemicals. So far CDC scientists have identified more than 250 different sources of food-borne illnesses in these two categories. Physical hazards are objects, such as glass or metal, that may enter foods accidentally during processing

Who's in Charge?

In the United States fifteen agencies oversee food safety and work to prevent food-borne disease. These include

- Food Safety and Inspection Service (FSIS): an agency of the U.S. Department of Agriculture. FSIS oversees the inspection, labeling, and packaging of meat, poultry, and eggs. It also oversees the importation of these products.

- Center for Food Safety and Applied Nutrition (CFSAN): part of the U.S. Food and Drug Administration. It oversees the rest of the food supply that is not covered by FSIS: seafood, produce, grains, beverages, etc. CFSAN also manages food labeling, supervises the HACCP program (see chapter 5), and has a bioterrorism prevention program. CFSAN also oversees food irradiation (a highly effective but controversial method of reducing pathogens).

- U.S. Environmental Protection Agency (U.S. EPA): sets limits on pesticides that can affect human health and manages water quality.

- Centers for Disease Control and Prevention (CDC): monitors and investigates health hazards, researches methods of prevention, and provides health education.

- State health departments: often the first contact with the public in a food-borne disease outbreak. They track and maintain data on outbreaks and communicate with other agencies. Health departments also educate the public about disease and often provide treatment.

or cooking. While physical hazards do not cause symptoms of disease, they must be prevented from entering our foods to ensure that they are safe to eat.

What are the sources of these hazards? In part they are a natural result of eating—humans (and other animals) have always encountered pathogens that are present in the environment. But some hazards are the result of our complex modern food system. It is like a huge city, with many "roads" through which food hazards can enter. According to the FDA:

> Factors that may affect the occurrence of such contamination include agricultural water quality, the use of manure as fertilizer, the presence of animals in fields or packing areas, and the health and hygiene of workers handling the produce during production, packing, processing, transportation, distribution, or preparation.

Imported food is another significant source of hazards, because it travels so far, passes through many hands, and is subject to different regulations between nations. Our tendency to gather in large groups also aids the spread of pathogens, which thrive in day care centers, schools, businesses, and other active settings. It is almost impossible for governments to block all of those roads. The best way to prevent "invasion" is for each of us to learn about food hazards and how they enter the human food chain. This knowledge gives us more power to protect our health.

Physical and Chemical Hazards

The risk with physical hazards is not illness but injury. Physical contaminants often enter the food chain during processing at factories. Two cases in 2008 provide unfortunate examples: a dairy company had to recall a batch of yogurt cups because they contained fragments of plastic and glass, and a candy company reported pieces of metal in their Valentine lollipops. Other physical hazards include stones, wood, dirt, and waste

Workers at this pasta-packaging factory wear hairnets to prevent contamination of the food.

from pests. Physical hazards usually get into food by accident, though sometimes it is the result of poor sanitation or lax inspections at a factory.

Chemical hazards cause illness by intoxication. These chemicals are of two types: toxic chemicals produced by organisms or natural or man-made chemicals. Many plants, bacteria, fungi (such as mushrooms, molds, and yeast), and other organisms produce toxins. For example, a brownish red color in water along ocean shorelines signals the bloom (rapid population growth) of certain toxic algae. Shellfish, such as oysters and clams, obtain food by filtering organisms out of water with their gills. An oyster that feeds on algae from these "red tides" will accumulate toxins in its body. People who eat infected oysters (or other shellfish) experience numbness, headache, dizziness, diarrhea, and other symptoms. This rapid onset of symptoms is called an acute response. Mercury, arsenic, and other naturally occurring chemicals can be equally toxic. Man-made intoxicants include chemicals used to grow crops, process food, and cook, as well as

This aerial view off the Gulf Coast of Florida shows an algae bloom, or "red tide."

The Canning Craze

In 1809 French chef and inventor Nicholas Appert discovered that food would last longer if it was heated inside corked glass jars. Appert's jars had to be filled and sealed by hand but were so popular that factory-sealable metal cans were soon developed. Canning didn't catch on in the United States until soldiers in the Civil War needed portable, preserved foods. Soon after, all kinds of foods were being canned.

Unlike the food kept in glass jars, however, you could not see the contents of cans. Consumers sometimes found that canned-food labels were deceptive. A study of canned foods conducted in

Chicago in 1874 revealed that some had been artificially colored. Others contained sawdust or worse unsavory materials. Chemicals were even added to conceal spoilage. This adulteration, or addition of foreign substances to food, was a widespread problem. In response the U.S. Congress passed the Federal Food and Drugs Act of 1906. It was described as "an Act for preventing the manufacture, sale, or transportation of adulterated or misbranded or poisonous or deleterious foods, drugs, medicines, and liquors, and for regulating traffic therein, and for other purposes."

Yet new forms of adulteration arose over the years. Some of them—including the use of preservatives, additives, and other chemicals—have become common and even accepted, despite the health risks they cause.

More recently adulteration has become a concern related to national security. The U.S. government continues to look at new ways to prevent intentional contamination of food and water. The Bioterrorism Act of 2002 attempts to reduce the risk of hazardous food being imported into the United States. This legislation supports the use of research, inspection, detection, prevention, treatment, and education to prevent food-related bioterrorism.

those used in packaging. They may sometimes cause an acute response but are also responsible for the development of chronic, or long-term, health conditions.

In 1564 Swiss alchemist and physician Paracelsus wrote, "What is not poisonous? Everything is poisonous yet nothing is poisonous. The dose alone makes the poison." His point was that any substance could potentially cause intoxication. Some substances (such as mercury) may cause illness at a very low dose—but increasing the dose of any substance will increase its effects. With this in mind the U.S. FDA and EPA regulate the amounts of certain chemicals that can be used in foods and on crops. Other chemicals that can affect food are also regulated. For example, mercury occurs naturally but is also released by the combustion of fossil fuels. Airborne mercury settles in water and then is passed up the food chain from microbes to larger animals. It can accumulate in humans who frequently eat fish and shellfish, causing damage to the nervous system and kidneys. (Developing fetuses are particularly at risk.) To reduce this risk, the U.S. EPA limits the concentration of mercury in drinking water to 2 ppb (parts per billion).

Microbiological Hazards

As mentioned above, some pathogens are considered chemical hazards because they cause intoxication. These pathogens invade a food source and then produce chemical wastes or toxins while consuming the food. Eating the food causes intoxication. A common source of intoxication is *Staphylococcus aureus*, a type of bacteria that thrives in dairy products and deli foods. This type of bacteria is easily spread by infected people who handle food.

Other pathogens cause infection. This occurs in two ways. Microbes can enter the body through a food or beverage and colonize the intestinal tract. This provides them with a steady source of food so they can multiply. Some species spread to other organs. Eventually, the body shows symptoms of infection. This is how *Salmonella* bacteria cause illness. Like many infective pathogens, these bacteria originate in feces. They can spread through soil and water onto

The burning of coal and other fossil fuels produces toxic chemicals such as mercury, which becomes integrated in the food chain.

many foods. When infected people fail to wash their hands after using the bathroom, the bacteria are transmitted onto surfaces and to other people.

A few pathogens produce chemical toxins after they enter the body. This is called toxin-mediated infection. It's less common but can be equally dangerous. One example is caused by the bacteria *Escherichia coli*, or *E. coli*. More than seven hundred strains of *E. coli* are known, some of which colonize the human body within hours after birth and are completely harmless. *E. coli* O157:H7, however, is a pathogenic strain of this bacteria; it is introduced through food that has

been contaminated with feces. Scientists sometimes refer to these bacteria as STEC, an acronym for Shiga toxin–producing *E. coli*. STEC were identified less than thirty years ago, in 1982, but the CDC believes they are responsible for approximately 70,000 infections each year in the United States.

Meet the Pathogens

Among the hundreds of potential food-borne hazards, a few crop up over and over again. This list includes some of the most common offenders and describes their vehicles and symptoms.

- There are two major groups of *Bacillus cereus* bacteria. One occurs in grain foods; the other is found in meats, fish, produce, and dairy. They cause intoxication that produces nausea, vomiting, abdominal cramps, and diarrhea.

- *Campylobacter* bacteria are found in such raw foods as milk, poultry, and meats; untreated water is another vehicle. They produce an infection with symptoms including bloody diarrhea, abdominal pain, fever, and muscle pain. Of the common food-borne bacterial infections, this one may hang on unusually long—up to ten days.

- *Clostridium perfringens* bacteria grow best in foods (especially meats) that are repeatedly heated, cooled, and reheated. There is a toxin-mediated infection after consuming *Clostridium*; symptoms include abdominal pain, nausea, and diarrhea that lead to dehydration.

- *Cryptosporidium* is a protozoan parasite. The inactive stage of these protozoa is called a cyst. Tiny cysts are passed through feces into soil or water, or spread to food or surfaces. Irrigation water may be contaminated with sewage, which infects produce. Other foods can be cross-contaminated by infected people. The infection is

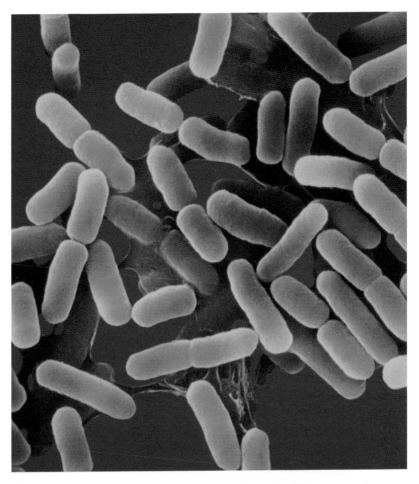

This image shows *E. coli* bacteria as seen through a high-powered microscope. If infected with a pathogenic strain, a person will experience abdominal pain, diarrhea, and nausea.

common in day care centers and causes watery diarrhea that leads to significant weight loss.

- *E. coli* O157:H7 (STEC) bacteria occur in meats, fish, and produce that have been exposed to feces or sewage. Infected people can act as vectors, moving the bacteria to foods and surfaces if they do not wash their hands well after using the bathroom. Undercooking

foods or washing produce poorly allows the bacteria to survive and infect the body, where they produce Shiga toxins. These cause extreme abdominal pain, nausea, and diarrhea with blood. Severe infection can eventually affect the kidneys.

- *Giardia lamblia* is another protozoan parasite. Like *Cryptosporidium* it forms cysts that are spread by water and soil. Worldwide, as many as 200 million people may be infected. Symptoms include diarrhea, nausea, gas, and weight loss.

- Hepatitis A is a virus that causes fever, nausea and vomiting, jaundice, and swelling of the liver. Symptoms can last for long periods and may be life threatening for people

Raw oysters are a culinary delicacy, but they can carry noroviruses and other pathogens that cause food-borne illness.

whose immune systems are already compromised. Infection occurs after eating raw shellfish or vegetables that have been exposed to contaminated water. This is the only food-borne illness for which a vaccine has been developed.

- *Listeria monocytogenes* bacteria are found in raw dairy products, meats, and produce. Infection produces symptoms similar to the flu—chills, fever, and aches—plus nausea and vomiting.

- Norovirus is a group of viruses that cause gastroenteritis—the classic seasonal "stomach flu"—with one to two days of nausea, vomiting, diarrhea, chills, aches, and fever. Raw shellfish and salad foods are usually the original vehicles, but norovirus quickly spreads to any food touched by an infected person.

- *Salmonella* bacteria thrive in raw meat and poultry, eggs, dairy products, and produce. Symptoms of infection are abdominal pain, headache, nausea, vomiting, and diarrhea leading to dehydration.

- *Shigella* bacteria infect dairy products, vegetables, and deli salads. These bacteria cause an infection with bloody diarrhea, fever, chills, and abdominal cramps.

- *Staphylococcus aureus* bacteria (Staph) produce intoxication, with some of the familiar symptoms of food-borne illnesses: nausea, vomiting, and abdominal pains. Victims will also experience changes in blood pressure and heart rate. Staph may grow in deli and precooked foods (including salted meats), salads, and dairy products.

- *Trichinella spiralis* is a parasitic worm in a group called helminths. These worms use humans and animals as hosts. The vehicle for *T. spiralis* is undercooked pork. Infection starts in the intestines and spreads to the muscles.

Mad Cow Disease

Some food hazards are hard to classify. Bovine spongiform encephalopathy (BSE), also known as mad cow disease, is one example. BSE is a cattle disease caused by prions, a type of protein found in the central nervous system. Normal prions in the central nervous system promote communication between cells. But some prions become damaged and misshapen; they're no longer able to do their job. Worse yet, healthy prions fold up when they come in contact with damaged ones. The result is a series of holes in the tissues of the central nervous system—basically, brain damage. BSE causes cattle to lose coordination as well as weight and, in the case of cows, to make less milk. The cattle may become irritable, nervous, or aggressive. Slaughterhouses test brain tissue for BSE, which is the only way to confirm infection.

BSE first appeared in the United Kingdom in the 1980s. It may have started when cattle were given feed containing sheep meat and bone that were infected with a prion-based disease. According to the CDC, the United Kingdom reported more than 184,000 cases of BSE between 1993 and 2007. To prevent the illness, in 1997 the FDA banned the use of mammal proteins in cattle feed. As of 2008, three cases had been confirmed in the United States, one each in the years 2003, 2004, and 2006.

Around the world approximately 150 cases of a related human illness, new variant Creutzfeldt-Jakob disease, have been reported. Infection results from eating parts of cattle that contain abnormal prions or consuming beef exposed to those tissues. Like BSE, this illness affects the nervous system and is incurable. Only two cases have been reported in North America, but travelers are advised to pay attention to food notices when visiting other countries.

An important realization about food-borne illnesses came in the early 1990s when the USDA conducted a study of ground beef. They took 563 samples from locations around the nation. In all cases the cattle had seemed healthy. But the samples showed a daunting variety of pathogens.

Campylobacter: found in 0.002 percent of samples

Salmonella: 7.5 percent

Listeria: 11.7 percent

Staphylococcus aureus: 30 percent

Clostridium perfringens: 53.3 percent

Raw ground beef has been shown to carry a variety of illness-causing pathogens.

In addition to these 78.6 percent of samples contained *E. coli.* These were not strains of *E. coli* O157:H7. However, the presence of any *E. coli* strain indicates that feces had contaminated the meat. The potential for food-borne illnesses was much higher than anyone had expected.

The data reinforced the concern that was felt after an event that had taken place in 1993, when a catastrophic outbreak of *E. coli* O157:H7 swept across several states in the western United States. Hundreds of people became ill, and many were hospitalized. Some suffered hemolytic uremic syndrome (HUS), a potentially fatal kidney disease. Several children died. The cause of the outbreak was undercooked hamburger from a large fast-food chain. In his book *Fast Food Nation: The Dark Side of the All-American Meal*, author Eric Schlosser reveals a fact that can easily be overlooked when dealing with food-borne illness outbreaks:

> Person-to-person transmission has been responsible for a significant proportion of *E. coli* O157:H7 illnesses. Roughly 10 percent of the people sickened during the Jack in the Box outbreak did not eat a contaminated burger, but were infected by someone who did. *E. coli* O157:H7 is shed in the stool, and people infected with the bug, even those showing no outward sign of illness, can easily spread it through poor hygiene. Person-to-person transmission is most likely to occur among family members, at day care centers, and at senior citizen homes. On average, an infected person remains contagious for about two weeks, though in some cases *E. coli* O157:H7 has been found in stool samples two to four months after an initial illness.

In other words, efforts to prevent food-borne illnesses can only be effective if they begin at farms and continue at every level, right to the kitchen table.

Three
Microbes and Humanity

For prehistoric people identifying safe foods must have involved a lot of trial and error. Watching other animals was helpful. Pigs turned out to be good taste testers—anything they ate safely would probably be edible for humans. And foods themselves may have provided invitations or warnings. For example, color, odor, and flavor indicate ripeness in plant foods. Food infected by bacteria may be discolored, have a softer texture, and smell bad. Prehistoric people must have learned to recognize and respect these signs.

But pathogens and toxins aren't always so obvious. They may occur in food without providing any indication of their presence—until the symptoms begin. One infamous example is the fungus *Claviceps purpurea*. Like other fungi—mushrooms, yeast, molds, etc.—*C. purpurea* reproduces by making spores that are carried on the wind or transported by insect pollinators. Spores infect the flowers of such grasses as wheat, barley, oats, and rye. Large growths called sclerotia appear on the plant. If harvesters do not notice the sclerotia, spores may become mixed with grains. When baked into foods and eaten, *C. purpurea*

The presence of ergot kernels (dark specimens) in harvested grain is evidence of infection by *Claviceps purpurea.*

produces an intoxication called ergotism. Some of the symptoms are common ones associated with food-borne illnesses, including nausea and vomiting. But victims may also experience hallucinations, feel like their arms and legs are itching, and have strong, uncontrollable muscle contractions. Ergotism is not common today, but several outbreaks occurred in Europe between 857 CE and the mid–1800s. Historically there have been periods when almost one-third of the grain harvest consisted of sclerotia, and thousands of people became ill at once. Back then people had no idea that a fungus could cause illness—and sometimes were not even aware it was in their food. As a result the symptoms of ergotism were often taken as a sign of mental illness or as evidence of demonic possession or witchcraft.

Illness or Evil?

In 1692 the quiet town of Salem, Massachusetts, was taken over by an unexpected kind of madness. It began when a young girl in the town, Betty Parris, showed a collection of odd behaviors: she squirmed and writhed as if in pain, hid from her family, and claimed to feel feverish. Soon, several of Betty's friends started to exhibit the same

symptoms. They claimed to have been bewitched by three women: an African-American slave and two white women. Instead of seeking help or denying the claim, the slave, Tituba, proclaimed that she was a witch. Soon other residents of the town were making accusations of witchcraft (left). Eventually, hundreds of people were thrown into jail. Twenty were executed before the furor finally died down.

Scholars have studied this case closely. There is evidence that many of the accusers made their accusations in order to gain property from the victims or because of religious or personal conflicts. Such petty jealousies may also be behind the European witch hunts of the sixteenth through nineteenth centuries. But some researchers believe there is another side to this story. Betty Parris showed classic symptoms of ergotism, as did many of the "bewitched" people in Europe.

The Germ Theory

It has taken a long time to understand the roles of microbes in nature and their relationship to human disease. Their existence was not even confirmed until the seventeenth century because before then no technology existed to observe such small objects. Then, in the 1660s and 1670s, two men discovered a whole new world.

Robert Hooke and Antonie van Leeuwenhoek were independent scientists, each with the same goal: to build more powerful microscopes. Famous for his variety of interests, Hooke was among the elite of English scientists. Using handmade microscopes, he became the first to identify plant cells and to observe small insects in detail. Leeuwenhoek worked in Holland, where he built tiny microscopes that revealed organisms even smaller than those seen by Hooke. Some of the organisms, which he called animalcules (Latin for "little animals"), were single-celled bacteria. Hooke and Leeuwenhoek both published their work, allowing scientists and citizens a first look at these organisms in all their strange and beautiful detail. Microscopes soon became an important scientific tool. Scientists and doctors used them to learn more about the human body and to observe animals, plants, and microbes. Yet even decades later, despite detailed observation, scientists found it hard to explain the lives of microbes. For example, many were convinced that microbes arose by spontaneous generation from decaying substances.

In the 1850s French winemakers went to chemistry professor Louis Pasteur with a serious problem: their fine wines were turning to vinegar. Pasteur examined the wine under a microscope. He found that normal (unspoiled) samples of wine contained great numbers of tiny, round yeast cells. In the spoiled wine few yeast cells remained, but there were many rod-shaped bacteria. Pasteur's observations revealed that yeast cause wine to ferment, which turns it to alcohol. He also learned that bacteria spoil wine by consuming the yeast. When the wine was heated gently, the bacteria died but the yeast survived. (This process is now called pasteurization and is used to kill bacteria in many foods.)

Louis Pasteur, French chemist and microbiologist, concluded that microorganisms cause food spoilage. The process of pasteurization, gently heating food, kills the organisms.

Pasteur realized that microbes—which he called "germs"—might also play a role in human illness. Until then illness had often been attributed to miasma, the foul odors that come from waste and decomposing matter. Alternatively, people were believed to suffer illness as a consequence of offending God. Pasteur developed a new "germ theory," which reasoned that diseases arise when pathogens multiply and spread between individuals. The theory was tested in two stages. First, Pasteur built an apparatus that filtered air through cotton. Little piles of dust gathered on the cotton. Under the microscope it was clear that some of the particles were actually microbes. When placed in a medium (a food source such as wine or broth), the microbe populations increased. In his scientific papers Pasteur concluded that microbes are present in the air

37

and explained that they "spring up and multiply from their respective germs"—in other words, microbes reproduce to make other microbes.

Microbes Everywhere

Like us, microbes need a source of energy to survive. This energy is obtained through the food chain. In most ecosystems sunlight is the original source of that energy. Plants, algae, and certain bacteria can use sunlight (along with carbon dioxide and water) to produce their own food (carbohydrates) through a process called photosynthesis. Organisms with this ability are called producers. Other organisms—including pathogens—must eat to obtain energy. These are called consumers, and they use many strategies.

- Herbivores eat producers. (Deer eat grass.)

- Carnivores eat other consumers. (Wolves eat deer.)

- Omnivores eat a mix of foods. (Coyotes eat deer and grass.)

- Scavengers eat dead organic material that is left in the environment. (Turkey vultures clean the carcasses of dead deer.)

- Parasites live on or in other organisms and obtain nutrients from their hosts. (Tapeworms are found in wolves' intestines. Worms and protozoa are common parasites, as are some bacteria and fungi and all viruses.)

- Detritivores are similar to scavengers but are smaller. They break down organic matter—such as dead leaves, bones, and feces—into small pieces. (Beetles, flies, worms, and millipedes are among the many animals that do this work.)

- Decomposers break down organic material into basic chemical elements that can be used again in the environment. (Many bacteria are specialized to decompose animal material, and a wide variety of fungi decompose dead plant material.)

Food-chain diagrams are simple models showing the flow of energy in ecosystems. But even the simplest is rarely a straight "chain." Instead, the complex feeding relationships in an ecosystem are more accurately described by a food web. In the example on the previous page we see that energy flows from Sun to grass, to deer, then to wolves, coyotes, and turkey vultures. Some energy passes on from the wolves to the tapeworms. More goes to the detritivores and decomposers.

Ecologists have shown that there are many beneficial microbes in nature in addition to those that act as decomposers. Cyanobacteria (photosynthetic bacteria) are a good example. These were among the first organisms on Earth. Their colonies, called stromatolites, began to form in oceans at least 3.5 billion years ago; fossil stromatolites can be found in

A marabou stork obtains its energy by scavenging the remains of a dead animal.

The Flow of Energy

The law of conservation of energy in physics says that energy is neither created nor destroyed. That holds true in ecosystems, as it does everywhere else in the universe. An ecosystem's energy often begins with light energy from the Sun. Producers convert this to chemical energy ("food"). From there it may be converted to kinetic energy (for motion), thermal energy (heat), or additional chemical energy in each organism. After many transformations most of the energy eventually returns to the environment as heat.

Producers receive a lot of energy from the Sun. But about 90 percent of this is "lost" as heat during energy conversions. The remaining 10 percent of the Sun's energy is stored in chemical bonds. These form the body of the producer. Herbivores can obtain this energy by eating producers, but they need to eat a lot of food to survive. This pattern continues up the food chain. That's why there will always be fewer zebras than grasses, and fewer lions than zebras.

South Africa and Australia. Not all modern cyanobacteria are benign; some produce toxins that can threaten human health if consumed. But early in Earth's history stromatolites played a key role for humanity. The planet's early atmosphere did not contain a great deal of oxygen. Through photosynthesis these organisms began to increase the concentration of this element in the atmosphere. Over time the atmosphere became suitable for the evolution of other forms of life. Remarkably, living stromatolite communities still grow in some shallow oceans.

Other bacteria play a vital role in the nitrogen cycle. Nitrogen gas makes up 78 percent of Earth's atmosphere and is required by all living things to build proteins. But animals and plants can't use nitrogen gas. Through a series of steps specialized "nitrifying" bacteria convert nitrogen gas to nitrate, which can be used by plants and passed up the food chain. Denitrifying bacteria drive the reverse process, converting nitrogen compounds back to a gas. Certain soil fungi, known as mycorrhizae, are essential to the growth of most plants. Approximately 95 percent of all vascular plant groups—including ferns, club mosses, gymnosperms (such as conifers), and angiosperms (flowering plants)—have these fungi on their roots. The plants and fungi exchange fluids: mycorrhizae suck up sugars made by the plants during photosynthesis, and plants obtain water and nutrients that mycorrhizae have absorbed from the soil.

Pasteur taught us that microbes readily colonize foods. This is often problematic, but in some cases it has interesting results. For example, the mold *Penicillium roqueforti* is a decomposer that grows naturally in soils. Cheese makers learned long ago that this mold thrives equally well in a vat of cheese curds. It breaks down complex molecules in the curds, producing simpler ones. Put aside the unappealing idea of having fungus in your food, and you can enjoy the product: tangy, delicious bleu cheese. In fact, many cheeses are made with the assistance of microbes. Similarly, yeast (another type of fungus) is necessary to make many breads and beers, while bacteria are used as starters for yogurt.

We often think of ecosystems on a grand scale: rain forests, grasslands, wetlands, and coral reefs are just a few

Some molds reproduce and thrive in cheese, producing a tasty product for consumption.

examples. But for microbes even the smallest animal or plant can qualify as an entire ecosystem. Like every other species, humans play host to a wide variety of microscopic flora and fauna, from dust mites that consume dead skin cells to amoebas that live between the teeth. Dr. Jeffrey Gordon of Washington University in St. Louis, Missouri, has estimated that 90 percent of the cells in the adult human body are not human but microbial. The digestive system seems to be a favored site of colonization, and studies indicate that each person's intestinal tract contains approximately one thousand species of bacteria. (The diversity varies, depending on an individual's health and diet, and may change over his or her lifetime.) Although pathogens may come and go, many bacteria in our intestines are commensal—they live quietly in our bodies, causing no harm or benefit. Some are even helpful to us, aiding the human immune system by fighting off pathogens. Relationships that benefit both partners are called mutualisms and are found in all ecosystems. Our mutualism with some intestinal bacteria appears so strong that when they decline or disappear, intestinal disorders may result.

Pathogens Love Civilization

Several characteristics of human civilization encourage the spread of microbes: we live in close proximity to one another, store large supplies of food, keep animals, and create a great deal of sewage. Why do microbes respond so well to these traits? As we've seen, our food is often also food for microbes. Humans can contract pathogens from animals, either by eating meat or living close to them. And our tendency to live close together means that pathogens can spread by direct contact, especially when good hygiene is not maintained.

For as long as people have lived in communities, sewage (bodily waste and other liquid wastes) has been a source of disease. In the earliest human settlements sewage was dumped into local bodies of water. This must have seemed like an easy solution to an ugly problem: the waste washes away or becomes diluted. But the same rivers and lakes used

for dumping often played a double role: as sources of drinking water. Sewage contributed pathogens that caused illness—both at the dumping site and downstream. Animal wastes caused a similar problem. Crops could become contaminated when sewage or manure was used as fertilizer.

Ancient people may not have made the connection between sewage and illness, but some recognized the need for clean drinking water. More than 2,500 years ago Egyptians added crystals of alum (iron sulfate or aluminum sulfate) to water in order to remove floating particles. In ancient India herbs were added to purify water. Water was also stored in copper containers (which kills bacteria) or filtered through particles of sand, copper, or iron. The Greek physician Hippocrates recommended straining water through a cloth bag before drinking. The Muslim physician Ibn Sina, who lived in the eleventh century, suggested boiling.

Yet these approaches were not universal. Waterborne illnesses were a worldwide problem until just a century ago.

This 1828 cartoon satirizes London's Metropolitan Water Supply as "Monster Soup."

During the nineteenth century thousands of people in the United States, Canada, and Britain sickened and died each year from diseases such as typhoid and cholera. After decades of study scientists and physicians solved the puzzle: the water had been contaminated by sewage, and the sewage contained pathogens that infected people. In 1850 the British government ordered that London's water be filtered through sand, and as a result, outbreaks of cholera became less frequent. In the United States water treatment did not become common until the early twentieth century. The nation's first water treatment plant was built in 1909 in Philadelphia, Pennsylvania. Four years later this plant pioneered another approach: it added chlorine, a disinfectant that is capable of killing pathogens.

This advance improved the health of millions. Yet even today, water and sewage mix frequently. When rainwater runoff flows over roads, farm fields, and other contaminated areas, it carries wastes and pathogens into the open channels and rivers that are used for irrigation. Treated wastewater is also used for irrigation. Wastewater is a combination of sewage and runoff. This water is sent to a treatment plant and put through different levels of treatment to remove pollutants and contaminants. Primary treatment removes larger solids from the wastewater. Secondary treatment is intended to break down many of the pathogens. Tertiary (third-level) treatment uses disinfectants to kill remaining pathogens, along with other techniques to remove heavy metals, nutrients, and other pollutants. The standard in tertiary treatment is for 95 percent of contaminants to be removed, theoretically making the outgoing water (effluent) clean enough to drink.

Globally, the use of wastewater and effluent in irrigation is widespread. In some parts of the world farmers have no other source of clean water—they must irrigate with completely untreated wastewater. In the United States the use of wastewater on crops is regulated at the state level. For example, California permits secondarily-treated water to be applied to crops that are used for animal fodder,

In many parts of the world treated and untreated wastewater is used in the irrigation of farmland.

fibers, and seed banks because these are not eaten. Other crops must be irrigated with water that has been treated at the tertiary level. Several cities have used the fertilizing capabilities of sewage as a way to keep sewage out of water, with mixed success. In Hanoi, Vietnam, sewage is diverted to fish farms, where it adds nutrients for the food chain in the ponds. This reduces costs for both the city and farmers, but it creates several new problems. The first is that wastewater reaching the farms is often a mix of sewage and industrial effluents. Chemicals may be taken in by the fish and then passed on to people who eat them. Second, farmers and consumers of the fish are exposed to pathogens from the wastewater. Eventually, practical uses of wastewater may be developed to help relieve the overload of sewage in growing cities. For now wastewater and effluent continue to present risks.

A second product, called sludge or biosolids, also comes from the wastewater treatment process. Biosolids can be sprayed onto fields in liquid form, injected below the surface of the soil, or dried and spread onto fields with a plow. There are two classes of biosolids. Class A cannot contain any detectable pathogens. Class B biosolids may contain pathogens, within limits. The pathogens in Class B biosolids are usually enteric. In other words, they occur in the human digestive system and are capable of causing foodborne illnesses. Among these are *E. coli*; *Campylobacter, Salmonella*, and *Shigella*; noroviruses; and parasites including *Giardia, Cryptosporidium*, and helminth worms. (See chapter two for more information on these pathogens.) To reduce the risk that these pathogens will be present on food when consumers purchase it, the U.S. EPA requires that crops must not be harvested for several weeks after spraying. Livestock also may not feed on a Class B–treated field for several weeks after treatment. Still, some researchers are worried about the use of biosolids. In 2000, 7.1 million tons (6.4 million tonnes) of biosolids were used in the United States. They were applied to approximately 1 percent of the nation's farm fields.

A tractor trailer unloads human biosolids, or Class B biosolids, on a farmer's field in Appomattox, Virginia.

Please Don't Pass the Pathogens

Sewage and its products—wastewater, effluents, and bio-solids—contribute significantly to the incidence of food-borne illnesses. But human mistakes also play an important role in transmitting pathogens. As the CDC explains:

Many foodborne microbes are present in healthy animals (usually in their intestines) raised for food. Meat and poultry carcasses can become contaminated during slaughter by contact with small amounts of intestinal contents. Similarly, fresh fruits and vegetables can be contaminated if they are washed or irrigated with water that is contaminated with animal manure or human sewage. ... Later, in food processing, other foodborne microbes can be introduced from infected humans who handle the food, or by cross contamination from some other raw agricultural product. ... In the kitchen, microbes can be transferred from another food by using the same knife, cutting board or other utensil to prepare both without washing the surface or utensil in between. A food that is fully cooked can become recontaminated if it touches other raw foods or drippings from raw foods that contain pathogens.

Good hygiene is among the simplest ways to prevent the spread of pathogens. In 2007 the American Society for Microbiology (ASM) commissioned a telephone survey asking about hand-washing habits. Ninety-two percent of those interviewed claimed to wash their hands every time they used a public restroom. There was a very different outcome in another survey conducted that year. More than six thousand travelers in four airports across the United States were observed as they left restrooms. Only 77 percent had washed their hands. Many people can't exercise this simple yet powerful choice to protect their health. The United Nations reports that 20 percent of the world's population has no regular access to safe water for drinking. Twice this many people have no reliable facilities for sanitation—they can't regularly use a clean indoor bathroom, wash their hands, or take a bath.

In 2002 a pandemic (worldwide outbreak) of severe acute respiratory syndrome (SARS) reached Canada. By July 2003 more than 250 people had become ill and 43 had died. SARS is caused by a virus that is spread via aerosol droplets (produced during fits of coughing or sneezing) in the air or on surfaces. If a healthy person comes in contact with the virus and then passes it to his or her mouth, nose,

49

or eyes, that person also becomes infected. Symptoms are mixed at first—aches, cough, and diarrhea—but often lead to pneumonia. That same year the ASM conducted a survey of hand washing at Toronto Airport in Ontario, Canada. It showed the impact of such an outbreak on people's hygiene habits. Only 3 percent failed to wash their hands before leaving the airport's restrooms.

It's understandable for people to show extra caution during an outbreak. But food-borne pathogens are tricky. Infected people may not show symptoms for days or weeks— yet the pathogen is passed out in their feces throughout that time. If those people fail to wash their hands, the pathogen easily spreads to others. That's why your own good hygiene shouldn't wait until someone in your family, class, or workplace becomes ill. For best success, remember what you learned in preschool:

- Wet your hands.

- Lather up! (Soap lifts dirt and other materials away from your skin. Antimicrobial soaps are not necessary; these may even be harmful, like antibiotics on farms, by creating resistance among bacteria in the environment.)

- Scrub! (Friction dislodges the materials in which pathogens hide.) Do the backs and palms of your hands, between your fingers, and under your nails. Sing the ABC song—in your head or out loud—or count slowly to twenty while you do this. That's how long it takes to do a really good job.

- Rinse! (Warm, running water is needed to thoroughly rinse your hands.)

- Dry! (Use a clean towel or a dryer. Don't scrimp here—pathogens grow well on damp surfaces. Properly dispose of paper towels and avoid sharing cloth towels in situations where others might be sick.)

Now you are less likely to pass the pathogens—but you could also pass along the habit. It may be a bit awkward at first, but friends, family, and coworkers will appreciate a gentle, funny, or educational reminder about the value of hand washing. It's not a perfect method of prevention—but it's a great head start.

Four
Our Changing
Food Chain

The end of the last Ice Age, about 12,000 years ago, contributed to a significant change in human culture. *Homo sapiens* had always been hunters and gatherers who moved through the environment in search of available food. Some people then settled into small communities. They began to grow their own food and to domesticate animals for meat. The earliest of these communities was located in the Fertile Crescent, a region encompassing southeastern Turkey and western Iran. Wherever the domestication of crops and animals took place, it offered the same benefits. Agriculture and animal husbandry provided a steady food supply and allowed people to increase their population. Larger populations provided safety from predators (and from rival humans), distributed the effort of producing food within a community, and eventually promoted trade and commerce.

Leaving the Farm
For millennia most people continued to live in communities in which their lives centered on farming. Even as civilizations grew up around the world, a great percentage

The First Crops

In 1997 DNA fingerprinting was used to determine that einkorn wheat—the ancestor of our modern wheat—was first domesticated in Turkey's Karacadag Mountains about 11,000 years ago. Many of the other "founder crops," which gave rise to foods cultivated and eaten by modern humans, also came from this same region in the Fertile Crescent. These include emmer (a wild form of wheat), barley, lentil, pea, chickpea (garbanzo bean), wild vetch (similar to lentil), and flax. Domestication of other important crops took place during this same time period in different parts of the world: maize in southern Mexico, rice in China and India, and root crops such as yams, sweet potatoes, and manioc in South America.

For thousands of years people ate whichever foods grew best in their local climate. European exploration in the fifteenth century changed that pattern forever. Sailors returned to Europe with a bounty of new foods to share. Corn, sweet potatoes, peanuts, tomatoes, and chili peppers were taste sensations. Some could not be grown in Europe. These were raised in Africa and imported to Europe.

of the population still worked the land to provide food. In the American colonial era settlers raised livestock and grew crops that included corn, grains, beans, peas, pumpkins, squash, cabbages, carrots, onions, and cucumbers. They used sweeteners such as sugar, molasses, and honey. Apples were popular, especially to make cider. Axes and hoes were their main tools, used to clear the wooded land and prepare the soil for planting. Tools we think of as common on old-fashioned farms—horse-drawn plows and handheld scythes for cutting grains—did not become part of the average farmer's collection until the 1750s. Despite the diversity of foods raised on farms, colonists continued to rely on many wild foods as well, including such large game as deer, waterfowl, small mammals, fish, shellfish, snakes, and turtles.

In colonial America people relied on their farms for food, using common hand tools to work their land.

The Industrial Revolution began in England during the 1700s with the invention of several machines that improved textile (fabric) manufacturing. Early in that century Thomas Newcomen introduced the steam engine. In 1769 James Watt modified Newcomen's design, making an engine that was much more powerful and efficient. The steam engine was first used to force water into mines, allowing metals to be extracted more quickly. Greater supplies of metal made it possible to build more machines, and coal provided an inexpensive fuel to run them. Watt's steam engine was soon modified for use in factories. Before long, citizens of Europe, the United States, and other nations were able to purchase a wide variety of products and tools that simplified their lives. Instead of being made by local blacksmiths or artisans, these were mass-produced in factories and transported from distant sources in steam-powered locomotives and ships.

Farmers' work was also changed by the Industrial Revolution. Traditionally, they had to cut grains by hand, then bundle them into large sheaves to dry in the sun. In 1831 Virginia inventor Robert McCormick devised a mechanical grain reaper that could be drawn by horses. His son, Cyrus, patented the design three years later, and it soon became widely used. (Modern combine harvesters are based on a similar machine, invented by Hiram Moore in 1835. Too large and expensive to appeal to nineteenth-century farmers, Moore's combine was adapted and reintroduced decades later. It's now an important machine on large fields, able to cut, thresh, and clean grain while leaving the straw separate.) Farmers in the 1800s also made use of steam-engine technology in cotton gins, rice mills, and sugar mills. Processing their crops mechanically was faster, which allowed them to handle larger crops and move them to market faster.

The focus of life in the United States and in some other nations began to change. Agrarian communities became smaller as more people moved into cities, and industry became the dominant force in human society. In its extensive website on agriculture the U.S. EPA gives a brief history of the changing role of farming in the United States since the colonial era:

In the mid–1800s farmers utilized machinery to help them harvest their crops. For instance, grain was cut with a mechanical reaper.

Growing crops for food was one of the first priorities of the earliest settlers arriving in North America. . . . In the era of Thomas Jefferson . . . farmers made up about 90 % of the work force. As late as 1900, almost 40 % of the labor force was engaged in producing crops and livestock for food, feed, and fiber. Now, with less than one percent of our population claiming farming as a principal occupation, most U.S. citizens have little or no crop production experience.

In her book *Kitchen Literacy*, historian Ann Vileisis explains how people's relationship with food was affected by the move into cities:

> Instead of spending days outdoors working in fields and gardens, greater numbers of Americans were spending their lives working indoors in factories, offices, shops, and homes. Though some city dwellers, especially the poorest, persisted in keeping small animals and gardens in back alleys, most had to delegate the work of procuring foods to market men and the fishermen and farmers who supplied them. In delegating this work, city dwellers were also relinquishing the opportunity to know their foods firsthand.

Farmers watched their produce sprout from seeds, collected their morning eggs from hens' nests, and raised the animals that would later become their meat. The work was constant, but it created an intimate connection with the food chain. City dwellers didn't have the burden of farmwork. But they became dependent on other people to provide healthy food. At first that food went directly from the farmer to the market. Over time it passed through an increasingly complex supply chain that involved warehouses, packing plants, factories, and distributors. And as supermarkets began to open in the 1920s, offering great volumes of food at lower prices, consumers' thoughts of the farm faded. Meanwhile, chemicals became a regular presence in the food production system. Farmers used them to grow more food, while manufacturers took advantage of their properties to make food last longer. Few people thought to ask whether this increasingly complex food chain would have an impact on their health.

Pests Be Gone

By the late 1800s populations in the United States and in some other nations had begun to increase so quickly that farmers were hard-pressed to meet the demand for food.

Feeding the Masses

Ecologists teach a principle called carrying capacity. It says that certain factors in the environment limit the size of populations. These limiting factors are unique to each population. They include components such as light, space, temperature—and food.

Human populations can also be affected by limiting factors. This happened about 70,000 years ago, when droughts in Africa caused the entire human population to decline to only 2,000 individuals. It took millennia for the population to recover. Until the Industrial Revolution began, food was one of the human population's most significant limiting factors. People generally had access only to foods that they grew, raised, or hunted; that they could trade with neighbors; or that were available in small local stores.

By 1800 there were one billion humans on the planet. Improvements in transportation, agriculture, and food production made more food available to more people. The human population doubled after just 127 years, reaching 2 billion in 1927. In 2009 the world population was almost 6.8 billion. (See graph at right.)

Climate scientists predict that by 2030 food may limit our population growth again. Due to global warming, certain parts of the world will be at greater risk of droughts that cause crop failure. Twelve regions are at particular risk. Most of these are in parts of the world where poverty is already a significant problem. The demand for biofuels may cause an additional concern because the variety most commonly in use, ethanol, diverts corn that would otherwise be used to produce meat and dairy products. This causes the cost of food to rise.

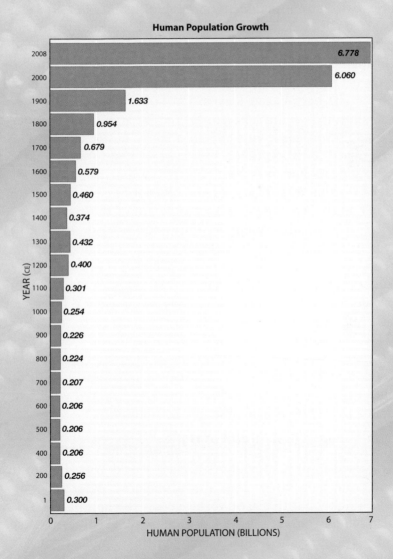

Human Population Growth

Source: Population Reference Bureau, http://www.prb.org.

Some farmers began to join together. This allowed them to share the expenses of farming equipment, labor, and shipping. They also concentrated on growing single crops, or monocultures. The larger crops benefited shoppers, who found that prices were lower and a greater variety of foods was available. But problems soon began to manifest. The first was an unanticipated increase in the number of pests.

Pests are a fact of life on farms. Historically, on small farms, chickens and other fowl were allowed to wander through the fields, eating insects. Farmers also handpicked bugs off plants or applied solutions made from ground walnut shells or tobacco leaves. On large monoculture farms infestations couldn't be controlled by such simple means. The solution came in 1885 in a spray bottle labeled "lead arsenate." This pesticide had an excellent success rate at killing pests and was particularly popular for use on fruit trees on the West Coast of the United States. Even in the nineteenth century people were aware of the risks of arsenic. A chemical element found in some rocks and soils, it was identified in the thirteenth century and had long been recognized as a poison that can affect the nervous system and other organs. (The effects of lead are more subtle because they accumulate over time, so they were not identified until the early twentieth century.) Despite the known risks, agricultural agencies encouraged the use of lead arsenate. Naively, some farmers assumed that if a little was good, a lot must be better. Fruit inspectors and health officials began to quietly confiscate produce covered with white dust—evidence of lead arsenate overspraying.

After decades of use, a new pesticide replaced lead arsenate. Dichloro-diphenyl-trichloroethane (DDT) was first used to protect soldiers during World War II from lice and from mosquitoes that spread malaria. After the war it was quickly put to use on farms across the nation. DDT was also widely advertised as a safe way to prevent insect infestations in the home. Thanks to the popularity of DDT, by 1950 pesticide sales had reached 300 million pounds (136 million kilograms).

To ward of ticks, a plane dusts a herd of sheep in 1948 with a powder that contains the pesticide DDT.

But the "miracle pesticide" was not really such a blessing. After the continual application of DDT to their fields, farmers needed to use even more—insect populations quickly developed resistance to it. This first became clear when houseflies in Denmark no longer responded to treatments. Similar examples of resistance began to occur among insect populations around the world. DDT and other organochlorine chemicals were also found to have properties that could affect human health and the environment. A broad-spectrum type of pesticide, they killed not only pests but also helpful insects such as pollinators. These chemicals also turned out to have a long life in the environment—and in people. Although insoluble in water, organochlorines dissolve in oils and can accumulate in body fats. They move along the food chain, becoming more concentrated in higher-level consumers. Few people other than scientists were aware of these dangers, however, and DDT use increased throughout the 1950s.

In 1962 ecologist and writer Rachel Carson published *Silent Spring* to warn the public about the dangers of DDT and other pesticides. She wrote:

> For example, fields of alfalfa are dusted with DDT; meal is later prepared from the alfalfa and fed to hens; the hens lay eggs which contain DDT.... The poison may also be passed on from mother to offspring. Insecticide residues have been recovered from human milk in samples tested by Food and Drug Administration scientists. This means that the breast-fed human infant is receiving small but regular additions to the load of toxic chemicals building up in his body. ... In experimental animals the chlorinated hydrocarbon insecticides freely cross the barrier of the placenta, the traditional protective shield between the embryo and harmful substances in the mother's body.... This situation also means that today the average individual almost certainly starts life with the first deposit of the growing load of chemicals his body will be required to carry thenceforth.

Activist and author Rachel Carson testified before a Senate Government Operations subcommittee in Washington, D.C., in 1963, urging Congress to curb the sale of chemical pesticides and aerial spraying.

Carson testified before the U.S. Congress in 1963, encouraging them to ban pesticides to protect nature and human health. Her words had a strong impact on some citizens and legislators, and DDT use declined slightly. The U.S. Environmental

63

Protection Agency finally enforced a ban in 1972, stating that DDT use had declined due to "increased insect resistance, development of more effective alternative pesticides, growing public and user concern over adverse environmental side effects—and governmental restriction on DDT use since 1969." Since then DDT has been recognized as a possible human carcinogen (cancer-causing substance). Despite this risk, as recently as 2006, WHO advocated its use in some parts of the world where malaria is rampant. In these cases the chemical's hazards must be weighed against the ravages of malaria. The challenge is to prevent DDT-tainted foods from these nations from being imported to regions where the chemical is banned, such as the United States.

Just as when lead arsenate went out of style, a new class of pesticides soon filled the gap that was left by DDT. Organophosphates seemed to solve the problems found with DDT. They do not move through the food chain, and they break down much more rapidly in the environment. However, organophosphates have a potent impact on the nervous system—so powerful, in fact, that they have been used as a nerve gas in several wars. Risks of poisoning from several of these pesticides, such as diazinon, were significant enough that the U.S. EPA instituted bans on them. Others are currently being phased out or are under review.

In the United States the federal government began its efforts to deal with pesticides through passage of the Federal Food, Drug, and Cosmetic Act of 1938 (FFDCA). This allowed the FDA to set tolerance levels (limits) on the amount of pesticide residues on food. Today, the U.S. EPA estimates that 80 percent of our exposure to pesticides comes through food. To control this risk, two laws—the FFDCA and the Federal Insecticide, Fungicide, and Rodenticide Act (FIFRA)—were amended in 1996. A new law was written to deal directly with pesticides. The Food Quality Protection Act (FQA) allows the U.S. EPA to oversee pesticide use. Pesticides must now be registered and, in most cases, tolerance levels are set to limit the amount of residue that can be left on food. Scientific studies are used to determine these tolerances, and limits are adjusted if new data reveal a health risk. This was clearly an important step. Since the FQPA was passed, more than a thousand different chemicals have been registered with the U.S. EPA for use as pesticides under thousands of different brand names.

Boosting Production

In the twentieth century population growth created a high demand for food. Farmers tried a wide variety of new methods to increase food production. One of the first approaches was to use more powerful fertilizers in the soil. Fertilizers provide additional nitrogen, which promotes plant growth. Traditionally, manure or "night soil" (human waste) was spread into the soil to provide this boost. In 1909 a German physicist discovered a way to fix nitrogen in the lab, as nitrifying bacteria do, to make ammonia. This product was first used as an explosive in World War I. When large supplies were left over after World War II, it was suggested for use as a fertilizer. Synthetic fertilizers (mostly made from natural gas) were soon put to use on farms across the nation. In some cases fertilizing caused more plants to grow in the same space. Other plants responded by producing more food. By selecting crops that responded well to fertilizers, farmers were able to increase their yield even more. The excess that was not needed for people, especially of corn and grains, provided a food source for animals. Animal producers were able to raise more livestock and poultry. Consumers benefited from this bounty of food as prices went down.

While this seems ideal, fertilizers create a number of environmental problems. Rain and irrigation water wash excess fertilizers off the soil and into nearby bodies of water, where the nitrates promote the growth of plants and algae. Such growth can increase populations of decomposing bacteria, which consume oxygen in the water, suffocating other aquatic life. Nitrates also enter the atmosphere. They can cause air pollution near the ground, contribute to acid rain, and break down ozone in the stratosphere (upper atmosphere). Air pollution contributes to respiratory

The Total Diet Study

Four times a year FDA scientists head out to grocery stores all over the United States. At each store they buy the same items—about 280 in all. These foods are prepared into diverse meals, such as those that frequently appear on American tables. But the meals aren't eaten. Instead, they are sent to FDA laboratories and tested for a variety of nutrients and chemical contaminants. The results are compiled into a report called the Total Diet Study.

The most recent Total Diet Study, completed in 2003–2004, compares the nutrient levels among these foods. It also reveals that many foods contain low levels of chemical contaminants and pesticides that may affect human health.

- Although lead was banned for use in paints and gasoline, residues remain in soil and can be passed to crops or water. Lead also occurs naturally in some rocks and is found in some insecticides, metal food cans, candy wrappers, and many other products. It can pass from a pregnant mother to a fetus, affecting brain development. Children who are exposed to lead over time, even at very low concentrations, may develop behavioral and learning differences. Adults can experience effects in many body systems.

- Malathion is an organophosphate pesticide that is in wide use, especially to kill mosquitoes. It affects the nervous system. Malathion can be found in forty types of foods, especially rices, breads, pastas, and cereals.

- Toluene is found in fossil fuel and is used in adhesives, rubber, and paint. It targets the nervous system and kidneys. Although toluene is not applied to food crops, the TDS found it in meats, dairy products, eggs, and grain-based foods.

- Benzene is made naturally in volcanoes and forest fires. It's added to dyes, detergents, and some plastics. It is also present in cigarette smoke and vehicle exhaust. Benzene slows down production of red blood cells, which transport oxygen. High levels of benzene in workplace air are linked to cancer among workers. The TDS identified benzene in forty-six foods. These included dairy products, meats, fish, fruits, vegetables, oils, water, and soda.

As the population grew in the twentieth century, farmers began to fertilize their crops to ensure a hearty yield.

health problems. Acid rain affects water quality and damages aquatic ecosystems. Stratospheric ozone helps to filter harmful ultraviolet radiation in sunlight; its depletion can cause skin cancer, cataracts of the eyes, and other health problems.

Antibiotics were another development of the mid-twentieth century. Producers began to worry about what would happen if a disease swept through the large and crowded feedlots and poultry houses. Their solution was to routinely give the animals low doses of antibiotics and antimicrobial chemicals in their feed. A side benefit of these chemicals was that the animals began to grow faster. By 1960, 1.2 billion pounds (544 million kg) of antibiotics were used to enhance the growth of livestock and poultry on farms in the United States. But since 1977 FDA scientists and many physicians have expressed concern that bacteria can become resistant to antibiotics after frequent exposure. In 1999 and 2000 several reports to the USDA strongly recommended reductions in antibiotic use—otherwise, these drugs may become less effective in treating human diseases. The USDA responded by engaging the services of the National Antimicrobial Resistance Monitoring System (NARMS). Since 1996 NARMS has collected weekly samples of important pathogens and toxins from animal feeding operations (AFOs) around the nation, where large groups of livestock or poultry are raised in close contact and used them to track trends in resistance. Meanwhile, the USDA and other agencies are collaborating on several goals. They seek new methods of testing and diagnosis, provide public education, and develop products such as vaccines and diagnostic tools.

As antibiotics became popular, another type of chemical was also being used to improve the success of AFOs. Hormones were first used on beef cattle, and in 1993 an enhanced version—recombinant bovine growth hormone (rBGH)—was introduced to dairy cows. rBGH is a genetically engineered version of the hormones made naturally by cows' pituitary glands. It has the potential to improve milk production by 25 percent or more, allowing dairy

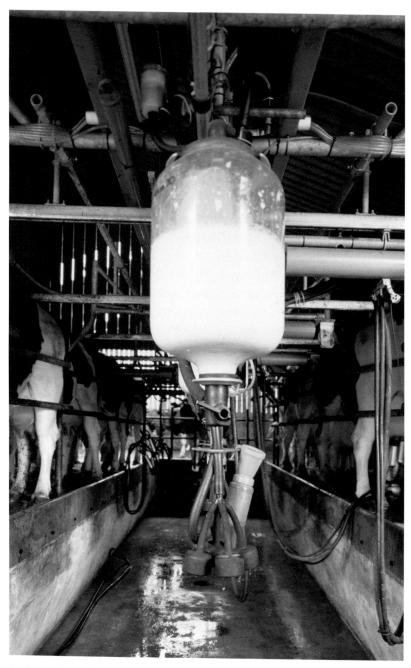

In the early 1990s growth hormone was introduced to dairy cows, allowing them to increase milk production by 25 percent or more.

farms to produce the same amount of milk using fewer cows. But there are trade-offs. Frequent use of rBGH can increase rates of mastitis, or udder inflammation, among dairy cows, which, in turn, requires antibiotic treatment. rBGH also stimulates cows to produce extra IGF-1 (insulin-like growth factor-1), a natural growth hormone. Humans also make IGF-1, but higher than normal levels appear to play a role in breast and prostate cancer among lab animals. Because IGF-1 is passed along in milk, it may increase this risk for humans. Children may be especially vulnerable because of their small size and high milk intake. The FDA maintains that rBGH-treated milk is safe, but the European Union has banned it, as have Japan, Canada, Australia, and New Zealand. As of 2008 each U.S. state was allowed to choose whether its milk required a label indicating that rBGH had been used in production.

Making Food Last

Each day Americans throw away enough food to feed 4 million people. This kind of waste is a very modern luxury that ancient people, and even our great-grandparents, would have found incomprehensible. Prehistoric hunter-gatherers learned tricks to preserve food so it lasted longer and could be carried from place to place. Drying is the oldest of these methods. (Modern scientists figured out that drying prevents spoilage because decomposers cannot grow without water.) Many cultures dried meats, fruits and vegetables, and beans by leaving them in the sun. Ancient Egyptians dried fish this way at least 14,000 years ago; dried seafood has also been found at archaeological sites in China and Japan. Foods also dry well when hung over a fire. Freezing and cold storage were equally effective in environments where such options existed. Snow, ice, and caves (most of which maintain remarkably stable temperatures throughout the year) provided excellent natural refrigerators, though they required people to remain in place or to revisit their food caches later. Seeds from staple crops such as wheat, millet, rice, and corn were roasted to make the grains more edible and long lasting. They

One of the oldest methods of preserving meat, fruit, and vegetables is drying them in the sun. This woman is drying apricots.

could later be ground into flour and meal to make bread, hard travelers' cakes, and other baked goods. Beans and peas simply had to be air-dried; when water was added, they recovered and made excellent soups.

Salts, sugar, honey, and vinegar have been used as preservatives for thousands of years. Ancient people may have only been trying out new flavors when they immersed foods in these substances and discovered their abilities to preserve by luck. It turns out that high-salt, high-sugar, and acidic conditions are also unsuitable for the growth of microbes.

The use of additives for flavoring, preservation, and food enhancement has become increasingly common over time. Currently, the USDA lists approximately 2,800 substances as food additives. These can be divided into several broad categories:

- nutrients—make food more healthful

- flavor enhancers—improve flavors already present in the food

- flavoring agents—add (or replace) missing flavors

- texture enhancers—add moisture and improve consistency

- sequestrants—preserve food with inactivate metals or acids

- colorants—replace colors lost in processing or provide "expected" colors

Sugar and salt are still among the most commonly used additives. Equally popular is high-fructose corn syrup (HFCS). Introduced in 1980 to replace sugar in soda, HFCS has become the most widely used sweetener in the United States and is now found in products as diverse as hot dogs, bread, and tomato paste.

The Food and Drug Administration requires that all products list their contents on the labels so that consumers are aware of the additives in the food they purchase.

In the early twentieth century the food industry was inundated with new additives. For the most part these were beneficial—they prevented spoilage, increased nutritional value, or made foods easier to cook. But a few turned out to be dangerous, increasing the risk of certain cancers or other health conditions. In response the federal government decided to regulate food additives. The Federal Food, Drug, and Cosmetic Act of 1938 required that all foods, beverages, and drugs have labels listing their contents and made it illegal to state the contents falsely. The Food Additives Amendment of 1957 supplemented this law. It required manufacturers to prove that their additives are safe for human use. This involves conducting lab tests to determine the toxicity, or effects, of a dose of the chemical. The risk of birth defects and cancer must also be evaluated. The FDA was assigned to regulate additives—they can approve or disapprove them and set safe levels for their use. In 1958 a special clause was added stating that foods that cause cancer in lab animals are prohibited from use in human foods. The 1960 Color Additives Amendment dealt with chemicals that add color (natural or synthetic) to foods. It says that manufacturers cannot use color additives to improve the appearance of unhealthy or unsafe food.

Conventional or Organic?

At the average supermarket there may be 45,000 different food items from which to choose. Many organic foods are now available alongside conventional brands. The Organic Foods Production Act of 1990 set national standards for how foods must be produced and handled in order to receive the official "USDA Certified Organic" label. The USDA describes organic food in this way:

> Organic food is produced by farmers who emphasize the use of renewable resources and the conservation of soil and water to enhance environmental quality for future generations. Organic meat, poultry, eggs, and dairy products come from animals that are given no antibiotics or growth hormones.

Consumers now have the choice of purchasing food items that are USDA certified organic.

Organic food is produced without using most conventional pesticides; fertilizers made with synthetic ingredients or sewage sludge; bioengineering; or ionizing radiation. Before a product can be labeled 'organic,' a Government-approved certifier inspects the farm where the food is grown to make sure the farmer is following all the rules necessary to meet USDA organic standards. Companies that handle or process organic food before it gets to your local supermarket or restaurant must be certified, too.

The Organic Trade Association reports that sales of organic foods have increased by 17 to 21 percent each year since 1997. By comparison total U.S. food sales have increased only 2 to 4 percent. Organics may never outsell conventional foods, yet many consumers consider it a positive step when farmers and manufacturers seek ways to reduce the number of chemical hazards that enter the food supply chain.

Five

Protecting Our Food Chain

Despite the best efforts of farmers, food companies, and the government, it's difficult to keep food safe. The food supply chain is massive, and so is our system for protecting it. In a 2007 report to the Government Accountability Office (GAO) and the House of Representatives, David M. Walker, former head of GAO, said:

> While this nation enjoys a plentiful and varied food supply that is generally considered to be safe, the federal oversight of food safety is fragmented, with 15 agencies collectively administering at least 30 laws related to food safety. The primary agencies are the U.S. Department of Agriculture (USDA), which is responsible for the safety of meat, poultry, and processed egg products, and the Food and Drug Administration (FDA), which is responsible for other food. In its many previous reports, GAO found that this fragmented system has caused inconsistent oversight, ineffective coordination,

and inefficient use of resources. For example: Existing statutes give agencies different regulatory and enforcement authorities. . . . Food recalls are generally voluntary. . . . Federal agencies are spending resources on overlapping food safety activities.

Walker recommended that the American food safety system be given the designation "high risk." This alerts law makers to give it special attention so that the system may be made more efficient and effective.

In 2001 the U.S. government decided to try a different approach, called risk analysis. It basically offers the "big picture" of a problem and uses a step-by-step method to address the risks involved. The FDA has adopted a risk analysis system called the Hazard Analysis and Critical Control Point (HACCP) program to improve the safety of seafood, beverages, meats, and poultry. HACCP was first developed in the 1970s to protect the safety of food for astronauts. Its goal is to prevent, eliminate, or reduce hazards rather than deal with problems after they begin. HACCP begins by analyzing the potential hazards to particular foods. Next, control measures are established. Critical control points (CCPs) are steps that make the control measure effective. For example, milk can be a vehicle for pathogens. Pasteurization is a control measure that can kill pathogens. Heating milk to 161 degrees Fahrenheit (72 degrees Celsius) is an effective CCP to ensure the effectiveness of pasteurization.

Each CCP is monitored, and strategies must be worked out in case a failure occurs. For example, if workers discover that milk samples still contain pathogens after pasteurization, the milk must be heated further or the equipment must be checked. The system is tested periodically at every step of the food supply chain, and all steps are documented. In a grocery store this might involve regular checks to ensure that refrigerator thermometers are functional and that employees know how to read them. In this process government agencies have also made a commitment to be transparent. This means they will share their data, policies, and any other information with the public.

Control measures have been put in place as a way to ensure food safety. This meat inspector checks the temperature of prepackaged ground meat.

Food Codes

Risk management and inspection are useful tools for managing food as it comes from farms, factories, and distribution centers. Experts have recommended that HACCP be used at all levels of the food chain. But restaurants, grocery stores, and institutions (such as nursing homes) have additional needs when dealing with food safety. In 1997 the FDA introduced the Food Code as a tool to guide them. The Food Code provides a set of uniform standards that are available to all retailers and institutions. It helps businesses solve and prevent problems and reassures consumers that anywhere they go, practices for food-borne illness–prevention will be consistent.

Food safety is a timeless issue and one that affects people around the world. Two international organizations realized this in the 1960s and worked to establish a food code that could be used by all nations. The organizations were the United Nations' Food and Agriculture Organization (FAO) and its World Health Organization (WHO). In 1961 they began to write the *Codex Alimentarius* (Latin for "Food Code"). The goal is for all nations to use the same practices to protect health and promote trade. The codex sets general standards to promote food safety. These deal with levels of pesticides, contaminants, and toxins allowed in food. It also sets standards for labeling. Codes of practice are suggested for food production, processing, manufacturing, transport, and storage. The codex also encourages the use of HACCP to detect and prevent hazards and has guidelines for identifying organic foods.

What Can You Do?
Everyone has a role on the human food chain, and we must each take responsibility to reduce the threat of spreading food-borne illnesses. Ideally, the goals of HACCP should be applied through the entire food chain, from farm to table. It may begin with farmers, factory and slaughterhouse managers, and food distributors, who have a responsibility to use methods that prevent contamination and transmission. Clearly, food service providers—from fast food to the finest restaurants—must ensure that kitchens are clean and that all employees exhibit a high level of hygiene. But this same level of care is also important in our homes. The CDC recommends a five-step plan to prevent food-borne illnesses: cook, separate, chill, clean, and report.

- Toxins may not respond to heat, but pathogens cannot survive it. Foods must be **cooked** until all parts are at a temperature of 160 °F (78 °C) or higher. Cook meat, poultry, and eggs all the way through—the center must also reach this temperature, and egg yolks should be firm.

- Prevent the spread of pathogens between different types of foods. In the refrigerator **separate** meats from dairy products and produce. Cross-contamination occurs when pathogens are moved from one location to another. To prevent this, use different cutting boards for meat and produce, and wash utensils in soap and hot water after each use. Raw foods must also be separated from cooked foods until they reach the dinner plate. People who are ill should also be separated from

You can take responsibility for reducing food-borne illnesses. When preparing a meal, separate foods and use designated cutting boards.

food. Because we don't always know when we are sick, there are two keys to handling food safety: proper hand washing (described below) for everyone and, for anyone who works with food, the use of gloves.

- Temperature has a strong effect on the growth of pathogens. CDC describes it this way: "Given warm moist conditions and an ample source of nutrients, one bacterium that reproduces by dividing itself every half hour can produce 17 million progeny in 12 hours." To prevent the uncontrolled growth of pathogens, foods should be **chilled**. This standard needs to be maintained in homes, refrigerated trucks and trains, warehouses, and all other locations where food is kept. While reporting on a nationwide outbreak of *E. coli* O157:H7 in bagged spinach, *The New York Times* noted that grocery store refrigerator cases are often kept as warm as 50 °F (10 °C), while the temperature required to prevent bacterial growth is 41 °F (5 °C). Freezers should be kept at 0 °F (–18 °C) or below. Shoppers need to think about this as they move around the store; perishable items should be purchased last. It's even wise to pick up produce near the end of the trip, to avoid bruising.

- *Listeria monocytogenes* can grow at very low temperatures—as low as 37 °F (3 °C)—so it's crucial to keep kitchens **clean**. Kitchen surfaces—counters, cutting surfaces, sinks, and others—should always be kept clean with detergent and water. The people who handle and eat food must be hygienic as well. Studies indicate that in nations where food- and waterborne-illness rates are extremely high, hand washing with soap can reduce infection rates as much as 47 percent. Several of the most contagious pathogens tend to spread simply through human-to-human contact in homes. Proper hand washing involves soaping the hands, rubbing them together briskly under warm, running water for at least twenty seconds, and then drying them with a clean towel for another twenty seconds. Hand sanitizers should not be used in place of washing with soap and warm water, but only as a temporary measure when soap and warm water are not available. Finally, foods themselves must be washed. Running water takes loose material off produce. Pathogens are most concentrated on the outer surfaces of fruits and vegetables, so it's important to take off outer leaves and skins.

- Food-borne illnesses can be difficult to diagnose. But whenever possible, cases should be **reported** to the proper authorities. Health agencies and the CDC track these. This makes it easier for them to recognize when an outbreak is under way.

Making a Change

Let's face it, food has become more than a way to fill your belly. The food chain can be a source of energy and nutrition, or it can be a pathway for disease. Each person plays a role

in promoting food safety. We do it by keeping our homes clean. We do it by making conscious and conscientious food purchases. And we do it by staying informed. Biologist Jane Goodall is an advocate for animals and people around the world. She offers some advice that's worth considering as we choose our foods each day:

> Yes, collectively we, the people, are the force that can lead to change. Every time we go shopping for food, every time we choose a meal in a restaurant, our choices—what we buy—will make a difference— not only for our own health and our own piece of mind, but also for the future of the planet.

Notes

Chapter One

p. 7, "...(CDC) received multiple reports of *Salmonella* infections.": Centers for Disease Control and Prevention, "Investigation of Outbreak of Infections Caused by *Salmonella* Saintpaul," 25 August. http://www.cdc.gov/Salmonella/saintpaul/ (accessed June 6, 2008).

p. 10, "In 2008 the earliest cases of salmonellosis were scattered...": Centers for Disease Control and Prevention (accessed August 25, 2008).

p. 10, "...a cluster of infections popped up simultaneously...": Weise, Elizabeth. "How Modern Science and Old-Fashioned Detective Work Cracked the *Salmonella* Case." *USA Today*, 17 June 2008. http://www.usatoday.com/money/industries/food/2008-06-17-tomato-outbreak-salmonella_N.htm (accessed June 18, 2008).

p. 10, "Approximately 2,300 strains (different genetic types)...": Smith, Tara. "A Focus on *Salmonella*." USDA Food Safety Research Information Office, December 2005. http://fsrio.nal.usda.gov/document_fsheet.php?product_id = 58 (accessed June 6, 2008).

p. 11, "...tomatoes had been linked to twelve outbreaks...": Herndon, Michael. "FDA Implementing Initiative to Reduce Tomato-Related Foodborne Illnesses." U.S. Food and Drug Administration, 12 June 2007. http://www. fda.gov/bbs/topics/NEWS/2007/NEW01651.html (accessed May 19, 2008).

p. 12, "...up to 90 percent of tomatoes are routinely moved...": Russell, Sabin. "Tomato 'Repacking' Vexes *Salmonella* Trackers." *San Francisco Chronicle*, 28 June 2008, p. B-1. http://www.sfgate.com/cgi-bin/article.cgi?f = /c/a/2008/ 06/28/BA9611GFS7.DTL (accessed June 29, 2008).

p. 13, "...raw chili peppers were the vehicle for transmission...": Jungk, J. et al. "Outbreak of *Salmonella* Serotype Saintpaul Infections Associated with Multiple Raw Produce Items— United States, 2008." *MMWR Weekly*, 29 August 2008. http://cdc.gov/mmwr/preview/mmwrhtml/mm5734a1. htm (accessed September 17, 2008).

p. 13, "During the 2008 outbreak more than 1,440 cases...": Center for Disease Control and Prevention (accessed August 25, 2008).

p. 14, "'Because many ill persons do not seek attention...": "Disease Listing: Foodborne Illness, General Information." Centers for Disease Control and Prevention, 25 October 2005. http://www.cdc.gov/ncidod/dbmd/diseaseinfo/ foodborneinfections_g.htm (accessed May 16, 2008).

Chapter Two
p. 15, "The United Nation World Health Organization...": "Food Safety and Foodborne Illness." World Health Organization, March 2007. http://www.who.int/media-centre/factsheets/ fs237/en/ (accessed May 18, 2008).

p. 15, "…1.8 million people die each year…": World Health Organization (accessed March 2007).

p. 15, "…76 million Americans contract food-borne illnesses each year…": U.S. Food and Drug Administration. *Food Code*. College Park, MD: U.S. Department of Health and Human Services, 2005. http://www.cfsan. fda.gov/~dms/fc05-toc.html (accessed May 18, 2008).

p. 15, "…more than 250 different sources of food-borne illnesses…": "Disease Listing: Foodborne Illness, General Information." Centers for Disease Control and Prevention, 25 October 2005. http://www.cdc. gov/ncidod/dbmd/diseaseinfo/foodborneinfections_g .htm (accessed May 16, 2008).

p. 16, "In the United States, fifteen agencies oversee food safety…": Walker, David M. "Federal Oversight of Food Safety: High-Risk Designation Can Bring Needed Attention to Fragmented System." U.S. Government Accountability Office, 8 February 2007. http://www.gao .gov/new.items/d07449t.pdf (accessed May 9, 2008).

p. 17, "'Factors that may affect the occurrence…": "Produce Safety from Production to Consumption: 2004 Action Plan to Minimize Foodborne Illness Associated with Fresh Produce Consumption." U.S. Food and Drug Administration, October 2004. http://www.cfsan.fda .gov/~dms/prodpla2.html (accessed May 20, 2008).

p. 17, "Two cases in 2008 provide unfortunate examples…": "Stonyfield Farms Announces Nationwide Voluntary Recall of Select 6-Ounce Fat Free Blueberry Yogurts." U.S. Food and Drug Administration, 28 March 2008. http://www.fda.gov/oc/po/firmrecalls/stonyfield03_08 .html (accessed May 20, 2008).

p. 19, "People who eat infected oysters (or other shellfish) experience…": Center for Food Safety and Applied

Nutrition. *Foodborne Pathogenic Microorganisms and Natural Toxins Handbook.* Washington, D.C.: U.S. Food and Drug Administration, January 1992, ch. 37. http://www. cfsan.fda.gov/~ mow/intro.html (accessed May 12, 2008).

p. 20, "In 1809 French chef and inventor Nicholas Appert...": Shephard, Sue. *Pickled, Potted, and Canned: How the Art and Science of Food Preserving Changed the World.* New York: Simon & Schuster, 2000, ch. 12.

p. 20, "A study of canned foods done in Chicago in 1874...": Vileisis, Anne. *Kitchen Literacy.* Washington, D.C.: Island Press/Shearwater Books, 2008, pp. 78–81.

p. 21, "...the U.S. Congress passed the Federal Food and Drugs Act of 1906.": "Federal Food and Drugs Act of 1906 (The 'Wiley Act')." U.S. Food and Drug Administration, n/d. http://www.fda.gov/opacom/laws/wileyact.htm (accessed May 18, 2008).

p. 21, "The Bioterrorism Act of 2002 attempts...": "Testing for Rapid Detection of Adulteration of Food." U.S. Food and Drug Administration, October 2003. http://www.fda.gov/oc/bioterrorism/report_congress.html (accessed May 27, 2008).

p. 22, "In 1564 Swiss alchemist and physician Paracelsus wrote...": Guggenheim, Karl Y. "Paracelsus and the Science of Nutrition in the Renaissance." *The Journal of Nutrition*, 1993, pp. 1189–1194. http://jn.nutrition. org/ cgi/reprint/123/7/1189.pdf (accessed September 25, 2008).

p. 22, "...U.S. EPA limits the concentration of mercury in drinking water...": "Consumer Factsheet on Mercury." U.S. Environmental Protection Agency, 28 November 2006. http://www.epa.gov/ogwdw/contaminants/dw_ contamfs/mercury.html (accessed December 19, 2007).

p. 23, "More than seven hundred strains of *E. coli* are known…": Todar, Kenneth. "Pathogenic *E. coli*." *Todar's Online Textbook of Bacteriology* (University of Wisconsin, Madison), 2008. http://www.textbookofbacteriology.net/ e.coli.html (accessed September 25, 2008).

p. 24, "STEC were identified less than thirty years ago, in 1982…": "*Escherichia coli.*" Centers for Disease Control and Prevention, 27 March 2008. http://www.cdc.gov/ nczved/dfbmd/disease_listing/stec_gi.html (accessed September 25, 2008).

p. 26, "Worldwide, as many as 200 million people…": "*Giardia: Drinking Water Fact Sheet.*" U.S. Environmental Protection Agency, September 2000. http://www.epa .gov/waterscience/criteria/humanhealth/microbial/ giardiafs.pdf (accessed May 18, 2008).

p. 28, "…the United Kingdom reported more than 184,000 cases of BSE…": "BSE (Bovine Spongiform Encephalopathy, or Mad Cow Disease)." Centers for Disease Control and Prevention, 13 February 2008. http://www.cdc. gov/ncidod/dvrd/bse/index.htm (accessed May 18, 2008).

p. 28, "…approximately 150 cases of a related human illness…": Bovine Spongiform Encephalopathy— Mad Cow Disease." U.S. Department of Agriculture, March 2005. http://www.fsis.usda.gov/FactSheets/Bovine_ Spongiform_Encephalopathy_Mad_Cow_Disease/ index.asp (accessed May 18, 2008).

p. 30, "…the USDA conducted a study of ground beef.": "Nationwide Federal Plant Raw Ground Beef Microbiological Study." U.S. Department of Agriculture, April 1996. http://www.fsis.usda.gov/Science/Baseline_ Data/index.asp (accessed May 23, 2008).

p. 31, "In his book *Fast Food Nation...*": Schlosser, Eric. *Fast Food Nation: The Dark Side of the All-American Meal.* New York: Harper Perennial, 2002, p. 201.

Chapter Three

p. 32, "Pigs turned out to be good taste testers...": Seperich, George J. *Food Science and Safety.* Danville, IL: Interstate Publishers, Inc., 1998, pp. 34–35.

p. 33, "Ergotism is not common today, but several outbreaks...": Hudler, George W. *Magical Mushrooms, Mischievous Molds.* Princeton, NJ: Princeton University Press, 1998, ch 5.

p. 33, "...almost one-third of the grain harvest consisted of sclerotia...": Hudler, ch. 5.

p. 34, "In 1692 the quiet town of Salem...": Linder, Douglas. "The Witchcraft Trials in Salem: A Commentary." University of Missouri-Kansas School of Law, March 2007. http://www.law.umkc.edu/faculty/projects/ftrials/salem/salem.htm (accessed May 19, 2008).

p. 35, "Betty Parris showed classic symptoms of ergotism...": Hudler, ch. 5.

p. 37, "Pasteur developed a new 'germ theory'...": Debré, Patrice. *Louis Pasteur.* Baltimore, MD: The Johns Hopkins University Press, 1998, ch. 7.

p. 37, "In his scientific papers Pasteur...": Pasteur, Louis. "The Physiological Theory of Fermentation." Louisiana State University Medical and Public Health Law Site, n/d. http://biotech.law.lsu.edu/cphl/history/articles/pasteur.htm (accessed June 1, 2008).

p. 39, "...stromatolites, began to form in oceans at least 3.5 billion years ago...": "Stromatolites and Prokaryotes."

Cushman Foundation, 4 November 2005. http://www
.cushmanfoundation.org/resources/slides/stromato
.html (accessed June 1, 2008).

p. 39, "...fossils can be found in South Africa and Australia.":
"Cyanobacteria: Fossil Record." University of California
Museum of Vertebrate Paleontology, 14 October 1995.
http://www.ucmp.berkeley.edu/bacteria/cyanofr.html
(accessed June 1, 2008).

p. 41, "...stromatolite communities still grow in some shallow
oceans.": Papineau, Dominic et al. "Composition and
Structure of Microbial Communities from Stromatolites
of Hamelin Pool in Shark Bay, Western Australia."
Applied and Environmental Microbiology, August 2005,
pp. 4822–4832. http://aem.asm.org/cgi/content/abstract/
71/8/4822 (accessed May 19, 2008).

p. 41, "Nitrogen gas makes up 78 percent of our atmosphere...":
"Nutrients in the Nation's Water—Too Much of a Good
Thing?" U.S. Geological Survey, 9 July 2001. http://water.
usgs.gov/nawqa/circ-1136/h7.html (accessed January
19, 2008).

p. 41, "...mycorrhizae, are essential to the growth of most
plants.": Royal Horticultural Society. "Underground
Partnership." *The Garden*, November 2003. http://www
.rhs.org.uk/thegarden/pubs/garden1103/mycorrhiza.asp
(accessed April 27, 2008).

p. 43, "...90 percent of the cells in the adult human body...":
Raloff, Janet. "Nurturing Our Microbes." *ScienceNews*,
1 March 2008. http://www.sciencenews.org/view/feature/
id/9433/title/Nurturing_Our_Microbes (accessed
September 25, 2008).

p. 43, "...each person's intestinal tract contains approxi-
mately a thousand species...": Mazmanian, Sarkis K.
"A Microbial Symbiosis Factor Prevents Intestinal
Inflammatory Disease." *Nature*, 29 May 2008, pp. 620–625.

p. 44, "More than 2,500 years ago, Egyptians added...": de Namor, A.F. Danil. "Water Purification From Ancient Civilization to the XXI Century." *Water Science & Technology: Water Supply*, 2007, pp. 33–39. http://www.iwaponline.com/ws/00701/0033/007010033.pdf (accessed May 18, 2008).

p. 45, "In 1850 the British government ordered...": de Namor, p. 36.

p. 45, "The nation's first water treatment plant...": "Urban Water Cycle: Water Treatment." City of Philadephia, n/d. http://www.phila.gov/water/urban_water_cycle.html (accessed October 22, 2007).

p. 45, "Globally, the use of wastewater and effluent in irrigation is widespread....": Hamilton, Andrew J. et al. "Wastewater Irrigation: The State of Play." *Vadose Zone Journal*, 2007, pp. 823–840. http://vzj.scijournals.org/cgi/content/abstract/6/4/823 (accessed June 1, 2008).

p. 45, "For example, California permits secondary-treated water...": Poole, Grant et al. "Soil, Water, and Crop Production Considerations in Municipal Wastewater Applications to Forage Crops." *Proceedings of the 2004 National Alfalfa Symposium*—University of California at Davis, 2004. http://alfalfa.ucdavis.edu/symposium/2004/ (accessed June 4, 2008).

p. 47, "In Hanoi, Vietnam, sewage is diverted to fish farms...": Furedy, Christine et al. "Reuse of Waste for Food Production in Asian Cities: Health and Economic Perspectives." The International Development Research Centre, 1 November 2004. http://www.idrc.ca/en/ev-30609-201-1-DO_TOPIC.html (accessed September 25, 2008).

p. 47, "There are two classes of biosolids.": "A Plain English Guide to the EPA Part 503 Biosolids Rule, Chapter 2: Land Application of Biosolids." U.S. Environmental Protection Agency, September 1994. http://www.epa.gov/owm/ mtb/biosolids/503pe/ (accessed May 23, 2008).

p. 47, "In 2000, 7.1 million tons…": "Guidance for Controlling Potential Risks to Workers Exposed to Class B Biosolids." Centers for Disease Control and Prevention, July 2002. http://www.cdc.gov/niosh/docs/2002-149/2002-149 .html#whatexp (accessed June 2, 2008).

p. 47, "They were applied to approximately 1 percent…": "Biosolids: Frequently Asked Questions." U.S. Environmental Protection Agency, 1 November 2007. http://www.epa.gov/OWM/mtb/biosolids/genqa.htm (accessed May 18, 2008).

p. 49, "'Many foodborne microbes are present in healthy animals…'": "Disease Listing: Foodborne Illness, General Information." Centers for Disease Control and Prevention, 25 October 2005. http://www.cdc.gov/ ncidod/dbmd/diseaseinfo/foodborneinfections_g.htm (accessed May 16, 2008).

p. 49, "In 2007 the American Society for Microbiology…": "Hygiene Habits Stall: Public Handwashing Down." *ScienceDaily*, 18 September 2007. http://www .sciencedaily. com/releases/2007/09/070917112526.htm (accessed September 27, 2008).

p. 49, "The United Nations reports that 20 percent…": "Student Conference on Human Rights: Background on Issues Relating to Water." Cyberschoolbus United Nations, 2005. http://cyberschoolbus.un.org/ student/2005/theme.asp (accessed September 20, 2008).

p. 49, "In 2002 a pandemic (worldwide outbreak) of severe acute...": "Summary of Probable SARS Cases with Onset of Illness from 1 November 2002 to 31 July 2003." World Health Organization, 31 December 2003. http://www.who.int/csr/sars/country/table2004_04_21/en/index.html (accessed September 20, 2008).

p. 50, "...hand washing at Toronto Airport in Ontario, Canada.": Hyde, Barbara. "American Society for Microbiology Survey Reveals That as Many as 30 Percent of Travelers Don't Wash Hands After Using Public Restrooms at Airports." American Society for Microbiology, 15 September 2003. http://www.asm.org/Media/index.asp?bid=21773 (accessed September 27, 2008).

Chapter Four

p. 53, "In 1997 DNA fingerprinting was used...": Heun, Manfred et al. "Site of Einkorn Wheat Domestication Identified by DNA Fingerprinting." *Science*, 14 November 1997, pp. 1312–1314.

p. 53, "...about 11,000 years ago. Many of the other 'founder crops'...": Diamond, Jared. "Location, Location, Location: The First Farmers." *Science*, 14 November 1997, pp. 1243–1244.

p. 53, "...maize in southern Mexico...": "Transition to Domestication." Minnesota State University eMuseum, n/d. http://www.mnsu.edu/emuseum/prehistory/latinamerica/topics/archaic_period.html (accessed May 19, 2008).

p. 53, "...rice in China and India...": Kiple, Kenneth F., and Kriemhild Coneé Ornelas. *The Cambridge World History of Food.* London, UK: Cambridge University Press, 2000, ch. 2.

p. 53, "...root crops such as yams...": Bray, Warwick. "Ancient Food for Thought." *Nature*, 9 November 2000, pp. 145–146.

p. 54, "Axes and hoes were their main tools...": Hurt, R. Douglas. *American Agriculture: A Brief History*. West Lafayette, IN: Purdue University Press, 2002, pp. 57–58.

p. 54, "...colonists continued to rely on many wild foods as well...": Miller, Henry M. "An Archaeological Perspective on the Evolution of Diet in the Colonial Chesapeake, 1620–1745," in *Colonial Chesapeake Society* (Lois Green Carr et al., eds.). Chapel Hill: University of North Carolina Press, 1988, pp. 176–199.

p. 55, "The Industrial Revolution began in England during the 1700s...": Strong, Roy. *The Story of Britain: A People's History*. London, England: Pimlico, 1988, pp. 307–331.

p. 55, "In 1831 Virginia inventor Robert McCormick...": "The McCormick Family and Their Mechanical Reaper." Leander McCormick Observatory Museum, 2008. http://www.astro.virginia.edu/research/observatories/26inch/history/reaper.php (accessed May 28, 2008).

p. 55, "Modern combine harvesters are based...": Hurt, pp. 145–146.

p. 56, "'Growing crops for food was one of the first...'": "Crop Production: Background." U.S. Environmental Protection Agency, 11 September 2007. http://www.epa.gov/oecaagct/ag101/cropbackground.html (accessed May 12, 2008).

p. 57, "In her book *Kitchen Literacy*...": Vileisis, pp. 42–43.

p. 57, "...as supermarkets began to open in the 1920s...": Vileisis, p. 160.

p. 58, "This happened about 70,000 years ago...": Associated Press. "Humans Nearly Wiped Out 70,000 Years Ago, Study Says." CNN.com, 24 April 2008. http://www.cnn.com/2008/TECH/04/24/close.call.ap/index.html (accessed May 10, 2008).

p. 58, "By 1800 there were one billion humans...": "Population Growth." Population Reference Bureau, n/d. http://www.prb.org/Educators/TeachersGuides/HumanPopulation/PopulationGrowth.aspx (accessed June 19, 2008).

p. 58, "In 2009 the world population was...": "World POPClock Projection." U.S. Census Bureau, 18 June 2008. http://www.census.gov/ipc/www/popclockworld.html (accessed May 8, 2009).

p. 58, "Climate scientists predict that by 2030...": Inman, Mason. "Warming May Cause Crop Failures, Food Shortages by 2030." *National Geographic News*, 31 January 2008. http://news.nationalgeographic.com/news/2008/01/080131-warming-crops.html (accessed May 13, 2008).

p. 60, "...on small farms chickens and other fowl...": Vileisis, p. 172.

p. 60, "The solution came in 1885 in a spray bottle...": Vileisis, p. 172.

p. 60, "...arsenic. A chemical element found in some rocks...": Barbalace, Kenneth L. "Periodic Table of the Elements: Element Arsenic, As." EnvironmentalChemistry.com, 2008. http://environmentalchemistry.com/yogi/periodic/As.html. (accessed June 3, 2008).

p. 60, "...by 1950 pesticide sales had reached 300 million pounds...": Vileisis, pp. 175–179.

p. 62, "...houseflies in Denmark no longer responded to treatments.": "Pesticide Timeline: DDT." U.S. Army Center for Health Promotion and Preventive Medicine, n/d. http://chppmwww.apgea.army.mil/ento/timefram/DDT.htm (accessed May 27, 2008).

p. 62, "In 1962 ecologist and writer Rachel Carson...": Carson, Rachel. *Silent Spring.* Cambridge, MA: The Riverside Press, 1962, pp. 22–23.

p. 64, "...a ban in 1972, stating that DDT..." "DDT Ban Takes Effect." U.S. Environmental Protection Agency, 31 December 1972. http://www.epa.gov/history/topics/ddt/01.htm (accessed January 23, 2008).

p. 64, "...as recently as 2006, the World Health Organization...": "DDT—A Brief History and Status." U.S. Environmental Protection Agency, 22 October 2007. http://www.epa.gov/pesticides/factsheets/chemicals/ddt-brief-history-status.htm (accessed January 23, 2008).

p. 64, "...the Federal Food, Drug, and Cosmetic Act of 1938 (FFDCA)." Vileisis, pp. 177–178.

p. 64, "...80 percent of our exposure to pesticides comes through food.": Fenske, Richard. "Organophosphates and the Risk Cup." National Ag Safety Database, March 2006. http://www.cdc.gov/nasd/docs/d001801-d001900/d001833/d001833.html (accessed May 23, 2008).

p. 64, "The Food Quality Protection Act (FQPA) allows the U.S. EPA...": "The Food Quality Protection Act (FQPA) Background." U.S. Environmental Protection Agency, 10 September 2007. http://www.epa.gov/pesticides/regulating/laws/fqpa/backgrnd.htm (accessed April 27, 2008).

p. 65, "Since the FQPA was passed, more than a thousand different chemicals...": "Assessing Health Risks from Pesticides." U.S. Environmental Protection Agency, 5 April 2007. http://www.epa.gov/pesticides/factsheets/riskassess.htm (accessed June 17, 2008).

p. 65, "In 1909 a German physicist discovered a way to fix nitrogen...": Pollan, Michael. *The Omnivore's Dilemma.* New York: The Penguin Press, 2006, pp. 41–43.

p. 66, "The most recent Total Diet Study, completed in 2003–2004...": "Total Diet Study: Summary of Pesticides and Industrial Chemicals Found in TDS Foods." U.S. Food and Drug Administration, 2008. http://www.cfsan.fda .gov/~comm/tds-toc.html (accessed May 7, 2008).

p. 69, "By 1960, 1.2 billion pounds...": Vileisis, p. 184.

p. 69, "In 1999 and 2000 several reports to the USDA...": Woteki, Catherine E., and Jane E. Henney. "USDA/HHS Response to the House and Senate Reports: Agriculture, Rural Development, Food and Drug Administration, and Related Agencies Appropriations Bill, 2000— Antibiotic Resistance in Livestock." U.S. Food and Drug Administration, 14 September 2000. http://www.fda. gov/cvm/Documents/jtrpt091400.pdf (accessed May 19, 2008).

p. 69, "...improve milk production by 25 percent or more...": Vileisis, p. 226.

p. 69, "Frequent use of rBGH can increase rates of mastitis...": Chilliard, Y. et al. "Recombinant Growth Hormone: Potential Interest and Risks of its Use in Bovine Milk Production," in *Biotechnology in Animal Husbandry* (R. Renaville and A. Burny, eds.). New York: Springer, 2001, p. 82.

p. 71, "rBGH also stimulates cows to produce extra IGF-1...": Malawa, Zea. "The Cancer Cow: A Study of the Risks Associated with rBGH Treated Cows." *Nutrition Bytes* (University of California at Los Angeles), 1 January 2002. http://repositories.cdlib.org/uclabiolchem/nutritionbytes/vol8/iss1/art4/ (accessed September 20, 2008).

p. 71, "The FDA maintains that rBGH-treated milk is safe, but...": "Frequently Asked Questions About rBGH: Our Position on Labeling and rBGH." Organic Valley Farms, 2008. http://www.organicvalley.coop/why-organic/synthetic-hormones/about-rbgh/ (accessed May 20, 2008).

p. 71, "Each day Americans throw away enough food...": Oliver, Rachel. "All About: Food Waste." CNN, 22 January 2008. http://www.cnn.com/2007/WORLD/asiapcf/09/24/food.leftovers/index.html (accessed April 25, 2008).

p. 71, "Ancient Egyptians dried fish this way...": Shephard, pp. 31–32.

p. 71, "Seeds from staple crops such as wheat...": Shephard, ch. 1.

p. 73, "Salts, sugars, honey, and vinegar have been used...": Shephard, ch. 2–7.

p. 73, "Currently, the USDA lists approximately 2,800 substances...": "Additives in Meat and Poultry Products." U.S. Department of Agriculture, November 2001. http://www.fsis.usda.gov/FactSheets/Additives_in_Meat_&_Poultry_Products/index.asp (accessed September 17, 2008).

p. 73, "These can be divided into several broad categories...": Seperich, ch. 9.

p. 73, "Introduced in 1980 to replace sugar in soda, HFCS has...": Pollan, pp. 102–104.

p. 75, "At the average supermarket there may be 45,000 different food items..." Pollan, p. 19.

p. 75, "'Organic food is produced by farmers...'": "What is Organic Production?" U.S. Department of Agriculture, June 2007. http://www.nal.usda.gov/afsic/pubs/ofp/ofp. shtml (accessed June 2, 2008).

p. 77, "The Organic Trade Association reports that sales...": "Organic Food Facts." Organic Trade Association, 2008.http://www.ota.com/organic/mt/food.html(accessed June 3, 2008).

Chapter Five

p. 78, "In a 2007 report to the Government Accountability Office...": Walker, David M. "Federal Oversight of Food Safety: High-Risk Designation Can Bring Needed Attention to Fragmented System." U.S. Government Accountability Office, 8 February 2007. http://www.gao.gov/new.items/d07449t.pdf (accessed May 9, 2008).

p. 79, "...the Hazard Analysis Critical Control Point (HACCP) program...": "HACCP: A State-of-the-Art Approach to Food Safety." U.S. Food and Drug Administration, October 2001. http://www.cfsan.fda.gov/~ lrd/bghaccp .html (accessed June 16, 2008).

p. 80, "In 1997 the FDA introduced the Food Code...": U.S. Food and Drug Administration. *Food Code.* College Park, MD: U.S. Department of Health and Human Services, 2005. http://www.cfsan.fda.gov/~ dms/fc05-toc. html (accessed May 18, 2008).

p. 80, "In 1961 they began to write the *Codex Alimentarius* ...": "Understanding the Codex Alimentarius." World Health Organization/Food and Agriculture Organization of the United Nations, 2006. ftp://ftp.fao.org/codex/ Publications/understanding/Understanding_EN.pdf (accessed May 24, 2008).

p. 81, "The CDC recommends a five-step plan...": "Disease Listing: Foodborne Illness, General Information." Centers for Disease Control and Prevention, 25 October 2005. http://www.cdc.gov/ncidod/dbmd/diseaseinfo/foodborne infections_g.htm (accessed May 16, 2008).

p. 82, "Given warm moist conditions and an ample source...": Centers for Disease Control and Prevention (25 October 2005).

p. 82, "...*The New York Times* noted that grocery store refrigerator cases...": Burros, Marian. "Tainted Spinach Brings Demands for New Rules." *The New York Times*, 27 September 2006. http://www.nytimes.com/ 2006/09/27/dining/27well.html (accessed May 11, 2008).

p. 83, "*Listeria monocytogenes* can grow at very low temperatures...": "*Listeria monocytogenes*." Center for Food Safety and Applied Nutrition. *Foodborne Pathogenic Microorganisms and Natural Toxins Handbook.* Washington, D.C.: U.S. Food and Drug Administration, January 1992, Ch. 37. http://www.cfsan.fda.gov/ ~ mow/ intro.html (accessed May 12, 2008).

p. 83, "...hand washing with soap can reduce infection rates...": Curtis, V., and S. Cairncross. "Effect of Washing Hands With Soap on Diarrhoea Risk in the Community: A Systematic Review." *Lancet Infectious*

Diseases, May 2003, pp. 275–281. http://www.ncbi.nlm.nih.gov/sites/entrez/ (accessed June 2, 2008).

p. 84, "Yes, collectively we, the people…": Goodall, Jane. *Harvest for Hope: A Guide to Mindful Eating*. New York: Warner Books, 2005, p. 284.

Further Information

Books

Bjorklund, Ruth. *Food-Borne Illnesses.* New York: Marshall Cavendish Benchmark, 2005.

Goodall, Jane. *Harvest for Hope: A Guide to Mindful Eating.* New York: Warner Books, 2005.

Kallen, Stuart A. (ed.) *Food Safety.* Farmington Hills, MI: Greenhaven Press, 2005.

Sherrow, Victoria. *Food Safety.* New York: Chelsea House Publishers, 2008.

Food Additives, from the Center for Science in the Public Interest
http://www.cspinet.org/reports/chemcuisine.htm
Interested in knowing which food additives are risky and which are safe? This site offers a thorough list of additives and their health effects. Banned additives are listed separately.

Food Safety, from the Centers for Disease Control and Prevention
http://www.cdc.gov/foodsafety/
Get the latest food safety warnings, along with data and educational information from the U.S. government's health agency.

Kids' Health: Food Safety
http://kidshealth.org/teen/nutrition/general/food_safety.html
This site offers background on how to avoid food-borne illnesses. It's perfect for sharing with friends, classmates, parents, and teachers who need a quick introductory lesson.

The Partnership for Food Safety Education
http://www.fightbac.org/
Fight Bac! is a collaboration between U.S. government agencies and professionals in food service, food science, and nutrition. This site offers a variety of valuable resources to teach the public about safe food handling in order to reduce the risk of food-borne illnesses.

Problems with Food Products: USDA Food Safety and Inspection Service
http://www.fsis.usda.gov/Fsis_Recalls/Problems_With_Food_Products/index.asp
This site explains how to report problems with bad meat, eggs, produce, or other foods that you have purchased from restaurants or retailers.

Bibliography

Carr, Lois Green et al. *Colonial Chesapeake Society*. Chapel Hill: University of North Carolina Press, 1988.

Carson, Rachel. *Silent Spring*. Cambridge, MA: The Riverside Press, 1962.

Center for Food Safety and Applied Nutrition. *Foodborne Pathogenic Microorganisms and Natural Toxins Handbook*. Washington, D.C.: U.S. Food and Drug Administration, January 1992.

Debré, Patrice. *Louis Pasteur*. Baltimore, MD: The Johns Hopkins University Press, 1998.

Ford, Brian J. *The Future of Food*. New York: Thames & Hudson, 2000.

Hudler, George W. *Magical Mushrooms, Mischievous Molds*. Princeton, NJ: Princeton University Press, 1998.

Hurt, R. Douglas. *American Agriculture: A Brief History*. West Lafayette, IN: Purdue University Press, 2002.

Kiple, Kenneth F., and Kriemhild Coneé Ornelas. *The Cambridge World History of Food*. London, UK: Cambridge University Press, 2000.

Pollan, Michael. *The Omnivore's Dilemma*. New York: The Penguin Press, 2006.

Renaville, R., and A. Burny, eds. *Biotechnology in Animal Husbandry*. New York: Springer, 2001.

Schlosser, Eric. *Fast Food Nation: The Dark Side of the All-American Meal*. New York: Harper Perennial, 2002.

Seperich, George J. *Food Science and Safety*. Danville, IL: Interstate Publishers, Inc., 1998.

Shephard, Sue. *Pickled, Potted, and Canned: How the Art and Science of Food Preserving Changed the World*. New York: Simon & Schuster, 2000.

Strong, Roy. *The Story of Britain: A People's History*. London, England: Pimlico, 1988.

U.S. Food and Drug Administration. *Food Code*. College Park, MD: U.S. Department of Health and Human Services, 2005.

Vileisis, Anne. *Kitchen Literacy*. Washington, D.C.: Island Press/Shearwater Books, 2008.

Index

Pages in **boldface** are illustrations.

Index

About the Author

Christine Petersen is a freelance writer and environmental educator who lives near Minneapolis, Minnesota. Petersen spent the first few years of her career studying the behavior of North American bats. Later, as a science teacher, she helped develop environmental education and service-learning curricula at an independent middle school. When she's not writing, Petersen conducts naturalist programs on bats and spends time with her young son. She enjoys snowshoeing, kayaking, photography, and birding. A member of the Society of Children's Book Writers and Illustrators, she is the author of more than two dozen books for young people.